Lhasa Apso Care G

Lhasa Apso Dog & Pupp

Facts & Information: Lhasa Apso, Puppies, Lhasa Apso Dog Price, Breeders, Grooming, Rescue, Temperament, Weight, Adoption, Personality, Size, Colors, Diet, Cost, Pictures and More

Deborah Heath & Mark Young

Copyright © 2015

International Standard Book Number:

978-1-910547-12-0

Acknowledgements

With grateful thanks to the many Lhasa Apso admirers out there who own or would like to own this wonderful breed. Without you, this book could not have gone from being an idea to becoming a formal book.

Finally, we would like to offer a great Thank You to the many dog breeders that have provided great knowledge of breeding and raising dogs over the years. Without your commitment, we would have no pedigree dogs today.

Thank You.

Table of Contents

Chapter One: Introduction

What does a fully-grown Lhasa Apso dog look like?

One of the most beautiful, unique, and joyful breeds in existence today, the Lhasa Apso is an independent breed of dogs that loves a challenge, and has been known to excel at agility events.

Fully-grown Lhasa Apso dogs measure approximately 27.3 cm or 10.7 inches high at the shoulder and have eye-catching long, straight hair.

There are many different Lhasa Apso grooming hairstyles to choose from, (for more information, refer to *Chapter Seven: Grooming, Cleaning & Clipping*) but their adult coat has a natural center-parting from top to tail, draping down to floor-length on each side.

Adult Lhasa Apso size

Before buying any puppy, it is a good idea to do some research on exactly how big the adult version of your chosen breed will grow.

In the excitement of seeing a tumbling tangle of playful puppies, it is easy to get carried away and imagine they will never grow too large for your home or garden.

Where space is limited, the petite Lhasa Apso dog is an excellent choice. This playful miniature breed will *never* surprise you, one day by leaping up, planting its paws firmly on your shoulders and giving your face a good *lick*.

Nor will it eat you out of 'home and home'. It is small enough to live in a flat with no garden, thrives in a town or country setting and is a hardy breed from Tibet.

The Lhasa Apso is an excellent watch-dog and will earn its keep by providing a useful 'early warning system' at the approach of strangers.

Which climates are suitable for Lhasa Apso dogs?

The breed is able to live in many different climates, but does best in cooler conditions, rather than tropical countries.

The original Lhasa Apso breed was developed in the harsh conditions of the highest mountains in the world, the Himalayas of Tibet. These icy mountains experience some of the Earth's most severe weather conditions, with extreme temperature changes from day to night.

Therefore, the Lhasa Apsos' heavy, long coat with a thick, under-layer, keeps these little dogs warm. In addition, the Lhasa's long, facial hair provides protection from the fierce sunlight, high winds and dust particles they encountered in their original habitat.

Hot humid climates are not good for a Lhasa Apso

Like a lot of dog-breeds, the Lhasa Apso does not do as well in hot, humid conditions. They can live in warmer climates as long as they have access to cool air from air-conditioning in the summer months.

Lhasa Apsos that live in very humid climates can have problems with fungal infections of the skin and ears. Dry heat is healthier for them and they do better in cooler climates.

At temperatures over 26 °C (80 °F), a Lhasa Apso will become lethargic and lose its appetite. Food consumption can drop by 25% - 50% and their general health may suffer.

Are Lhasa Apsos hard to train?

Yes, they can be. Not for any lack of intelligence, but because of their independent nature.

They are not focused on pleasing their owner and successful obedience training requires a lot of patience, persistence and a sense of humor.

However, a well-trained Lhasa Apso is a wonderful companion that will bring love, loyalty and lots of fun into any owner's life.

The History of the Lhasa Apso

Few breeds offer a more interesting background than today's pedigree Lhasa Apso dog-breed. The history of the Lhasa Apso goes back so far in time that it is an integral part of Tibet's folklore.

In ancient Tibetan mythology, the country's protector was the mighty, 'Snow Lion'. It was believed that the Snow Lion lived on the high mountain peaks of the Eastern Himalayas, shrouded in clouds, where humans had never set foot.

The Snow Lion was viewed as a youthful creature, full of vibrant energy and a sense of joy. It also symbolized courage and the ability to overcome all obstacles.

These traits were all present in the, 'lion-maned', Lhasa Apso dogs, and it was believed they were the powerful Snow Lion's earthly representatives, sent to watch over their homes.

While the huge Tibetan Mastiff was bred to guard the outside of homes and monasteries, the Lhasa Apso was developed to provide an additional watch-dog inside the home.

Over 2,000 years of breeding

Bred for over 2,000 years to make useful indoor watchdogs, the original name for the Lhasa Apso was *Abso Seng Kye.* This means, *the lion sentinel that barks.*

Sometimes this is also translated as *goat-like barking sentinel* (from the word, *rapso,* meaning, *goat-like,* referring to the Lhasa Apso's *beard.*)

Both translations are likely to be correct, as no doubt different Tibetan villages had their own (similar) names for this popular dog over hundreds of years.

At home anywhere

Although many writers insist on referring to the Lhasa as 'aristocratic' and 'regal', believing they were the jealously-guarded, precious possessions of the Tibetan upper-class, this is not completely accurate.

According to Lhasa breeders in India, that have spent time in Tibet, the lively Lhasa Apso was - and still is - a much-loved family pet.

This ancient, 'early-warning' system was popular with villagers, land-owners, nobles *and* the isolated monasteries set high on the mountain peaks.

How the Lhasa Apso breed reached the west

Until the Chinese invasion in the 1950's, the country was ruled by the Buddhist monks, and the head-of-state was the Dalai Lama.

In 1933, the naturalist and world traveler, Charles Suydam Cutting visited the country as part of the U.S. government's Central Asian expedition of 1928 - 29.

The 13th Dalai Lama, from his monastery/palace in the capital city of Lhasa, presented Cutting, with a 'good-will' gift of a pair of locally-bred Lhasa Apsos.

The role of Charles Suydam Cutting

Charles S. Cutting was the owner of the Hamilton Farms Kennel in New Jersey and introduced the Lhasa Apso dog-breed to America upon his return in 1933.

The breed's current name is usually attributed to the name of the capital city, 'Lhasa' and the Tibetan word, 'apso' meaning long-haired.

The Lhasa was admitted to the American Kennel Club (AKC) around 1935, solely through Cutting's success in breeding from the original dogs.

It was, however, wrongly classified as a 'terrier' before being re-classified into the Non-Sporting Group in 1959.

Lhasa Apso breed in 1920's London

The Lhasa Apso is just one of a number of Eastern breeds to come to Britain early in the 19th century. The first Apsos arrived in the U.K. in the early 1920's and were being shown in London soon after.

In 1933, the Lhasa Apso dogs were admitted to the British Kennel Club, in the Utility Group. The 'Utility' classification is used to identify ancient breeds, originally bred as working dogs, whose special 'job' is no longer necessary.

However, the Lhasa did not become widely popular in the U.S., the U.K. and around the world until the late 1970's and 80's.

Chapter Two: Understanding the Lhasa Apso

Physical characteristics

Proud and jaunty

The Lhasa Apso has an attractive upright carriage. With head held high, the Lhasa always looks bright and alert.

They are agile little characters that will delight you with their lively movements and the swish of a luxuriant, plumed tail.

Long body shape

You can also recognize a Lhasa Apso dog by its long body length, which evolved to house an extra-large pair of lungs.

In the high-altitude conditions of the lofty Himalayas, the 'thin' air has less oxygen than at ground level.

Powerful lungs allowed this energetic little dog to breathe in enough oxygen to thrive in his mountain home.

Independent temperament

This little dog's nickname is, 'lion-dog', and not only because of its abundant 'mane' of head and facial hair. Lhasa Apsos have a lively and independent spirit. They also have a reputation for being quite stubborn on occasions, too.

However, they are also loyal and affectionate pets that love to be mischievous and play outdoors. To get the best from your Lhasa puppy, you will need to undertake training right from the start.

In addition to the usual house-training, Lhasas need firm obedience training to learn you are the leader of the pack, and social training with other dogs. You will find detailed training instructions in Chapter Nine which covers the area of training your Lhasa Apso.

Lhasa Apso personality traits

According to both the UK Kennel Club and the American Kennel Club, these are the main personality traits you can expect from a correctly-bred Lhasa Apso dog:

1) Intelligent, independent and stubborn - benefit from early training

2) Acute hearing

3) Suspicious of strangers – a major Lhasa Apso personality trait making it an excellent indoor watch-dog

4) Energetic and playful with friends/family – but only recommended for homes containing adults or older children

5) Lhasas will nip younger children who handle them awkwardly or annoy them

6) The Lhasa is not a 'lap dog' and should not be confused with the Shih Tzu breed from China

7) Will happily run for miles with owners who enjoy walking or hiking

8) Highly valued as loyal and affectionate companions, puppies and Lhasa Apso rescue dogs are popular pets.

Male Lhasa Apso – Height & weight

Officially, the breed standard for male Lhasa Apso dogs is 27.3 cm (10 ¾ inches) measured at the *withers*. (The *withers* is the prominent ridge between the shoulder blades and the highest point of a Lhasa's body.)

A healthy Lhasa Apso male should weigh between 14 – 16 lbs. (6.4 – 8.2 kg).

Female Lhasa Apso – Height & weight

Female Lhasas are slightly smaller than the male in height and should weigh between 12 – 14 lbs. (5.4 – 6.4 kg).

Appearance

Both male and female breed standards require dark-brown eyes and a black nose, (except liver-colored Apsos, which may have a brown nose).

Kennel Club breeding experts are dedicated to improving a breed by 'breeding out' genetic health problems and maintaining the dog's physical characteristics in balance.

They create official, 'breed standards', to describe each breed's correct physical appearance and personality.

Although the wording of the standards may differ slightly from one country to another, the international standards are more or less the same.

The breed standard and selecting a healthy Lhasa Apso

When inspecting Lhasa Apso puppies for sale, or a Lhasa Apso rescue dog for adoption, knowing the breed standard is an important tool to help you find a healthy, well-bred dog.

It is easier to evaluate the strengths and weaknesses of adult Lhasa Apso rescue dogs than puppies, as their physique and personality are fully developed.

Choosing a future 'show' dog

Choosing the best puppy to be a prize-winner is not an easy task. If you are selecting a puppy to enter dog-shows, or looking for a particular color in the pup's adult coat, it is a good idea to get some advice from a breed expert.

Only an expert can inspect a puppy and give you a clear idea of how it will look when it grows its adult coat.

Sometimes, unscrupulous puppy-breeders advertise puppies from litters sired by a winning male show-dog and provide the correct papers to prove this.

However, if the stud-dog is a prize-winner, but the mother has not been screened for illness, she will not be Kennel Club registered. Therefore, there is no guarantee the pups will be healthy and unregistered dogs are not allowed to appear in pedigree dog-shows.

Many first-time buyers have ended up with a sick dog, instead of a prize-winner owing to this trick. Going to dog shows and joining your nearest Lhasa Apso breed club will put you in contact with experts in the breed.

Official Breed Standards: AKC/The Kennel Club

Character: Gay and assertive, but wary of strangers. ('Gay' means 'cheerful, happy, and full of joy'.)

Size: Variable, but about 25 cm to 28 cm (10 inches to 11 inches) at shoulder for males (dogs), with the females (bitches) slightly smaller.

(K.C. Size: Ideal height: dogs: 25 cm (10 inches) at shoulders; bitches slightly smaller.)

Color: All colors equally acceptable with or without dark tips to ears and beard.

Body Shape:

The length is measured from the high-point of shoulders (*the withers*) to the high-point of the buttocks.

The length should be *longer than* the height at the withers (*withers* refers to the bony ridge between the shoulders).

Well ribbed-up, strong loin, well-developed quarters and thighs.

(K.C. Body Shape: Length from point of shoulders to point of buttocks greater than height at withers. Ribs extending well back. Level top-line. Strong loin. Balanced and compact.)

Coat: Heavy, straight, hard, not woolly nor silky, of good length and very dense.

(**K.C. Coat:** Top coat long, heavy, straight, hard - neither woolly nor silky. Moderate undercoat. Coat never impeding action.)

Mouth and Muzzle:

The preferred 'bite' is either level or slightly undershot. Muzzle should be of medium length; a square muzzle is objectionable.

Head:

a) Heavy head furnishings with good fall over eyes

b) Good whiskers and beard

c) Skull narrow, falling away behind the eyes in a marked degree, not quite flat, but not domed nor apple-shaped

d) Straight foreface of fair length

Nose:

a) Black

b) Length from tip of nose to eye to be roughly about one-third of the total length from nose to back of skull

Eyes: Dark brown, neither very large and full, nor very small and sunk.

Ears: Pendant, heavily feathered.

Legs: Forelegs straight; both forelegs and hind legs heavily furnished with hair.

(**K.C. Hindquarters:** Well developed with good muscle. Good angulations. Heavily furnished with hair. Hocks when viewed from behind parallel and not too close together.)

Feet: Well feathered, should be round and cat-like, with good pads.

(K.C. Feet: Round, cat-like with firm pads. Well feathered.)

Tail: Well feathered, should be carried well over the back in a screw shape; there may be a kink at the end.

(K.C. Tail: High-set, carried well over back but not like a pot-hook. Often a kink at the end. Well feathered.)

Carriage: A low carriage of stern is a serious fault.

Note: i) 'Feathered' means 'feathery hair' in the breed standard description. ii) 'Stern' is the front, under-section of the body like the human chest area.

(K.C. Gait/Movement: Free and jaunty)

K.C. Note: Male animals should have two apparently normal testicles fully descended into the scrotum.

The Kennel Club - Lhasa Apso faults

Here is the section on faults issued by the U.K. Kennel Club:

"Any departure from the foregoing points should be considered a fault, and the seriousness with which the fault should be regarded, should be in exact proportion to its degree, and its effect upon the health and welfare of the dog and on the dog's ability to perform its traditional work."

For the ease of understanding, I have broken down this quote into points:

1) In the judging rules for pedigree dog shows, any departure from the breed standard is considered to be a *fault*.

2) Small departures from the breed standard will lose fewer points than large differences.

3) However, the *degree of fault* – i.e. whether it is a small, medium or large fault - is judged directly on how much the fault:

a) affects the health and welfare of the show-dog and

b) affects the dog's ability to perform its traditional work or utility or sport.

Puppies' coat color changes

As the Lhasa Apso puppy matures, its coat will change in color, texture and length. When you are choosing a puppy to buy, it can be difficult to know what the adult color will be.

Insiders examine the puppy's hair at the roots to see if it is a different color from the rest of the hair. When the roots are a different color, it is likely that the puppies coat color will change as it matures.

Lhasa Apso color range

The Lhasa Apso dog-breed has many different colors and coat patterns/markings. The 'Breed Standard' of The Kennel Club U.K. and the American Kennel Club (AKC) accepts them all.

Lhasa Apso Colors and Markings - AKC

a) Black - Black & tan – Blue - Charcoal - Gray – Grizzled

b) Cream – Golden - Red - Red gold

c) Liver - Silver – White

Markings

a) Black Mask with tips

b) Brindle

c) Parti-color (this refers to large or small white patches)

d) Sable - Black tips

e) Sable with white markings

f) White Markings

Definition of grizzled

The word, 'grizzled', refers to a coat that has a mixture of black and a lighter color. For instance, a 'red grizzled' coat would be black with red and a 'black grizzled' coat is a combination of black and white hairs.

There are many beautiful brown colors, too, which are known as cream, golden, red-gold and red.

The AKC 'alternative' colors

The 'alternative' Lhasa Apso colors are grey, silver, liver, charcoal and blue. These are softer versions of the standard colors or less common types of 'grizzle'.

For instance, 'blue' in a Lhasa Apso coat would be a faded black shade. Silver is actually a 'grizzled' shade, made by a combination of cream with blue or black hair.

Lhasa Apso markings

The Lhasa Apso also has a variety of eye-catching patterns and markings, which are greatly admired at shows.

The AKC recognizes a variety of coat patterns and markings, which can vary greatly in individual dogs.

1. Black mask with tipping

This describes Lhasa Apso dogs which have a black beard and black-tipping on another part of the body.

Some dogs have only a little black beard, while others may have a full black mask, reaching up to the eyebrows.

2. Brindle

Brindle is a striped marking with a mix of light and dark bands of color in the coat. Although the Lhasa Apso brindle colors are not as vivid as a tiger's stripes, they create a similar impression – especially if you catch sight of a brindled Lhasa from the corner of your eye.

The most common brindle colors are black and silver, black and brown and blue and cream.

3. Parti-color

Parti-color really means 'patches of color' in modern English, so parti-color and white marking would be random patches of white both on the Lhasa's head and body.

For example, some mainly white dogs have a darker underbelly and legs that are covered in small 'splashes' of white. Or a Lhasa could have just a patch of white on its chest, with matching dainty white toes.

4. Sable/Black tipping

'Sable' and 'black-tipping' refer to lighter hair, which deepens to a dark color at the tips. This creates an attractive color-ripple effect as the dog moves around.

Lhasa Apso Colors and Markings - The Kennel Club

The Kennel Club colors are known as brown, golden, honey, sandy, slate, smoke, parti-color, black and white. All are accepted as standard colors with equal merit.

Lhasa Apso Breed Ranking & Annual Registration Figures

a) AKC currently rates the Lhasa Apso at No. 63 in *Top 100 Most Popular Dogs*.

b) The Kennel Club registered approximately 3,500 Lhasa Apsos in 2014.

Chapter Three: Buying a Healthy Lhasa Apso Puppy

Buying a Lhasa Apso puppy that's healthy and happy can only be achieved by researching local, professional breeders often affiliated with breed clubs.

If there are none in your area, you may have to travel to other parts of the country.

However, it's well worth the effort to find a responsible dog breeder and here's why.

Avoid puppy-farms and amateur breeders

A puppy-farm is the last place to go for a healthy dog. They are nothing more than puppy-factories where the health of the dogs is far less important than financial profit.

Puppies are often taken from their mothers as early as 8 weeks old and sold to pet shops or other agencies that then sell the Lhasas through internet websites and newspaper adverts.

Lhasa Apso puppy farms and back-yard breeders have no love or respect for dogs. They breed Lhasa Apso puppies continuously, ruining the health of the mothers and often producing pups with serious genetic medical conditions.

How to find a responsible breeder

To find a healthy, pure-bred Lhasa puppy with a good temperament requires research. You can start with the lists of breeders supplied by these organizations:

a) The Lhasa Apso Breed Club

b) The Kennel Club

c) American Kennel Club

d) Regional Affiliated Clubs

If you don't find a 'good' breeder with a Lhasa Apso puppy for sale immediately, don't be discouraged.

The process of getting a healthy pedigree puppy can take a little time, but nothing is more important than getting a well-bred dog. You can also find healthy puppies like this:

a) Contact the Secretary of a Lhasa Breed Club who will be able to give you some names and contact details of breeders in the club

b) If you can, visit a show where Lhasa Apsos are being exhibited, talk to the exhibitors and get answers to your queries

c) Consult the list of Lhasa Apso breeders in the *Resources* section.

How much do Lhasa Apso puppies cost?

In the U.K., a Kennel Club registered Lhasa Apso puppy currently costs from £500 to £700. Breeders usually expect a non-returnable deposit of £50 to £100. This deposit helps with ensuring that the purchaser is genuinely committed to owning a Lhasa Apso, while filtering out those that are not.

In the U.S. an AKC registered puppy costs approximately $750 to $850 and you will also be asked to provide an appropriate financial deposit.

If you see an advert for a Lhasa at a much cheaper price, this will probably be a dog 'with no papers'. This means you are not dealing with a responsible breeder and the dogs have not been health tested before mating.

Build a relationship

Potential owners, who can show they know how to look after a carefully bred Lhasa puppy, will be more likely to be offered one.

Even if a breeder does not currently have a litter for sale, they may be planning a litter in the next few months. It is quite normal to be put on a waiting-list for a pedigree puppy.

Keep in touch with your chosen breeder and use the, 'waiting-time', to prepare your home and read all about caring for your puppy.

Inspecting the kennels

You should also check the hygiene standards of the breeder's kennels, as good breeders will have a clean environment for their dogs and pups. Go to the breeder's location, if you are able to, and make sure it is clean.

Observe how the breeder and dogs behave around each other. If the dogs show any signs of being wary or cringing away from the breeder, this is a sign of bad treatment that can lead to puppies having behavioral problems.

If there is currently a very young litter at the breeder's kennels, you won't be able to visit until the pups are older. This is the correct way to prevent the transmission of infection or disease to the pups.

However, apart from that, you should be able to go and see Lhasa Apsos and their home environment. If the site is dirty and the dogs are living in poor conditions, cross this breeder off your list.

Poorly managed kennels produce puppies that grow up to have many health and behavioral problems.

Healthy dogs

Remember that nursing mothers will look a little 'frayed around the edges', especially if they are nursing a large litter. Nursing mothers tend to lose weight and their coat thins after they produce a litter and feed several puppies.

However, the rest of the dogs should look healthy and they should have good levels of energy. It is important not to look at just the parents of the puppies but at all of the dogs.

If any dog looks unwell, don't forget to ask the breeder about its condition.

Both parents should be Kennel Club registered

Ask if *both* of the parents of the puppy you are offered are Kennel Club Registered. If they are not both registered, you will not be able to register the puppy in your name.

In addition, if the breeder allows your dog to be bred, you will not be able to register any of the resulting litter as pedigrees unless both parents are registered.

Check for dew claws

Remember to ask the breeder about feeding, worming and whether the puppy has had the preliminary vaccinations. Ask if the puppy has *dew claws* as this is often overlooked.

Dew claws are little, vestigial toes that grow high up on a dog's paw. If they are firmly attached and sticking out causing problems for your dog, then they can be removed by a vet.

Puppies should have been raised indoors

While Lhasa Apsos do enjoy time outside, it is important for the *socialization* and health for all puppies to be raised in the home.

Puppies that live indoors, recognizing a human as the leader of the pack, will be more or less home-trained and accustomed to people and other dogs.

Early socialization by a good breeder can save you a lot of training-time and headaches later.

What the breeder expects of you

At the same time, you can expect a breeder to be asking you questions and checking out your references.

Dog breeders put a lot of time, effort, money and love for the breed into producing each healthy litter of puppies. They are very cautious about whom they will allow to buy a Lhasa Apso puppy.

If the breeder gets any negative feelings about you, they will probably refuse to sell you a puppy. You have to convince the breeder that you will provide a wonderful home for one of their puppies.

Be prepared to answer a lot of questions about yourself and your knowledge of the Lhasa breed. If you have a regular vet for other pets, ask her/him to write you a reference.

Finding a breeder

Ensure that you thoroughly research any breeder that you may be interested in – including those listed in Chapter Fifteen (under the Resources section),or on kennel club websites. It can happen that someone, who was an excellent breeder in the past, has changed their life-focus and is not as reliable as before.

Every litter should have a goal in mind that will further the breed and you should ask the breeder to explain their breeding plan.

Responsible breeders will be delighted to explain their breeding plan to you. However, bad breeders will not know what you mean by this question.

Essential documents you should insist on receiving at the conclusion of the sale:

A Contract of Sale – clearly showing the responsibilities to the puppy of both the Breeder and the Buyer.

i. The contract should also list any official Kennel Club endorsements (restrictions) that the breeder has placed on the puppy's records.

ii. In particular, it should be stated on what basis the breeder may be prepared to remove the endorsement.

iii. You must give a signed acknowledgement of any endorsement placed on the Contract of Sale, either before or at the time the sale is officially completed.

1) Written advice on training, feeding, exercise, worming and immunization.

2) A pedigree document detailing the dog's ancestry.

3) This could be hand-written or a printed pedigree from the breeder *or* an official one from the Kennel Club.

4) The Kennel Club/American Kennel Club and the British Veterinary Association offer canine health schemes, which aim to detect and monitor certain inherited conditions.

5) There are also some DNA tests now available for certain breeds. Ask which vaccinations your puppy has had and which ones are still required.

6) Copies of any additional health certificates for both the dam *and* the sire.

7) Temporary Insurance certificate. The breeder should offer you 4 weeks free Kennel Club/AKC Pet Insurance for your new puppy, which starts from the moment you collect your puppy.

8) Check this has actually been set up and do not leave until you have the Certificate of Insurance in your hand. This cover is important, should your new puppy suffer from any illness or injury before you have time to take out long-term insurance.

Note: 'Endorsements' are actually 'breeding restrictions' that the breeder may place on the puppy's records.

For example, this could be, 'not for breeding' if there is a high risk of passing on a genetic medical condition. Even though the puppy may not be suffering from the condition, it could be a 'carrier' of a disease or other medical condition.

Alternatively, an older Lhasa Apso female could be past the age of breeding, which is 7 years of age. Other endorsements may include, 'not for export'.

Note: Never complete a sale with a breeder that promises to 'send the documents on to you later'.

Can I trust breeders accredited by the UK or American Kennel Clubs?

Not always, I'm afraid. Unfortunately, there are many Lhasa puppy breeders on the assured/accredited lists compiled by the UK Kennel Club and American Kennel Club, and others that have *not* been properly checked recently.

Obviously, the Kennel Clubs do not have the money to pay for frequent expert checks and they offer their 'recognized breeders' lists as a guide *only*.

All such lists carry a warning that clears the publishing-club of any responsibility for the health or quality of the dogs sold by breeders on the list.

So when it comes to buying a puppy, remember the phrase: "Buyer beware"

How can I tell who is a respectable breeder?

First of all, have a chat with the person offering Lhasa Apso puppies or rescue dogs for sale, in person or by phone. Asking the right questions will quickly reveal the genuine Lhasa Apso breeding experts from the rest.

A full list of questions to ask the breeder can be found at the end of this chapter, but here are some of the main questions to ask right from the start:

1. Can I see the puppy's living quarters and its mother?

Always insist on viewing the Lhasa puppy in its home and along with its mother, to see how it behaves. Good breeders will always be happy to do this, as they are keen to get to know *you* and see how you interact with their much-loved Lhasa pups.

Respectable sellers will want to check that you are going to be a responsible dog-owner, able to provide the best care and training to one of their carefully bred puppies.

2. Can I see the dog's pedigree documents/details of the previous owner?

Reputable breeders will always have the necessary paperwork ready to show purchasers. These include a record of the puppy's blood-line or, in the case of a rescue Lhasa Apso, the name and phone number of the previous owner.

If you buy from anyone who cannot provide the official paperwork you will be taking a big financial risk and encouraging the cruel treatment of dogs.

3. Can I see the GPRA (Unaffected) Eye Test Certificates?

In particular, you should ask for a GPRA (Unaffected) Eye Test Certificate. This is an essential document proving that a Lhasa Apso puppy or rescue dog has been tested for Generalized Progressive Retinal Atrophy (GPRA).

GPRA is an eye disease passed down to Lhasa Apso pups from an affected mother, father *or* grandparents. Genuine breeders work hard to 'breed out' unwanted genetic diseases. They will be pleased you have asked this question and shown your interest in the dog's good health.

A good breeder will definitely have the (Unaffected) Eye Test Certificates which prove the pups and their parents have been tested and certified free of GPRA.

4. What if the seller says he doesn't have the health-check certificates?

Then it is not recommended to buy from them. The simple rule here is, "no documents – no sale". 'Puppy-farmers' and 'back yard' breeders don't test for genetic diseases in breeding pairs, and mate Lhasa Apso dogs at random.

Discovering your Lhasa Apso has a genetic disease - because you wanted 'a cheap one' or were in a hurry - is not only expensive in vet's bills; it can be emotionally taxing.

Summary:

1) Inspect the puppy's living quarters 'at home' with mother

2) Ask for breeding records and health check documents

3) Ask for GPRA 'Unaffected' Eye Test Certificates

4) Never buy pups of less than 8 weeks old

5) Never buy pups from pet shops or from people who advertise online or in newspapers

Breeder Interview Questions

Once you select a breeder, phone and have a chat during which you can ask a few of these questions:

1) How long have you been breeding?

2) Are you an affiliated breeder of The Kennel Club/American Kennel Club or any other Lhasa Apso club?

3) When was the last time your premises were inspected by an official from the Kennel Club?

4) What are the breed standard characteristics?

5) What is the standard Lhasa Apso temperament?

6) What are the main health problems for this breed?

7) Do you carry out health screenings on breeding pairs before breeding a litter?

8) Can you give me a copy of the blood-line breeding documents and a full set of health-screening certificates?

9) How much exercise does a Lhasa Apso need as a puppy and as an adult?

10) Do Lhasas bark a lot?

11) Does this breed shed its hair seasonally?

12) How often does a Lhasa Apso dog need to be groomed?

13) What are the best training methods for a Lhasa Apso puppy?

14) At what age does puberty usually begin?

15) How long before s/he acts like an adult dog?

16) Is this breed safe with young children?

17) Does this breed get along well with other pets?

18) Will there be any 'endorsements' on the Contract of Sale?

19) Do you have an overall breeding plan or do you just like breeding puppies?

20) Do you show your dogs at The Kennel Club/AKC events?

In the United States and the U.K. the Lhasa Apso health certificates include tests for these conditions:

a) Eyes Certified by a board-certified ACVO Ophthalmologist

b) OFA or Penn Hip certification for Hip Dysplasia

c) OFA evaluation for Autoimmune Thyroiditis

d) OFA evaluation for elbow dysplasia is optional in the breed

Ask for copies of all of these certificates, or the U.K. equivalent, plus Kennel Club registration documents.

Approaching show-dog breeders online

Many Lhasa Apso dog breeders, especially people who breed for dog shows and as a hobby, have web sites so they can show off their dogs.

They may have a litter of puppies occasionally, but when they get an e-mail from a stranger asking, "How much to buy one of your dogs?" they are likely to be offended and suspicious.

They may think the person wants to do something terrible to their precious puppies, like use them at a puppy farm. They will usually ignore that kind of message or send a cool-toned reply.

However, breeders of show dogs are exactly the ones that have the best quality puppies. If you want to contact a show or hobby breeder and enquire about a litter, it is important to follow the social niceties.

Do not begin by asking the price. Instead, tell them you are looking for either a pet, or a show-quality puppy, if you intend to show the dog. Ask if they have any puppies or if they know of a responsible breeder they can recommend.

Note: Enquiries from people who show some knowledge of the breed and its value as a pet, watch-dog or show-dog will get offered the best puppies.

Chapter Four: Getting Ready for a New Puppy

Cost of Dog Ownership

The price of your puppy is not the only expenditure you need to consider. Lhasa puppies need good quality food and veterinary care, starting with vaccinations that need to be repeated annually.

Vaccinations

Most breeders will advise you to take your new puppy to the vet within 2 – 3 days of taking him home. This is good for you, the breeder and the puppy. If you have a legal contract with the breeder, it probably includes this as 'condition of purchase'.

It is important to make sure the puppy is in good health when he arrives at your home. Depending on the puppy's age and its vaccination schedule, you may be able to combine its next vaccinations with his first vet check-up.

Recommended vaccinations vary slightly, depending on where you live. However, the standard puppy vaccinations in Britain include the following:

1) Canine Parvovirus

2) Canine Distemper

3) Canine Parainfluenza Virus

4) Infectious Canine Hepatitis

5) Kennel Cough

6) Leptospirosis

Coronavirus vaccination is optional. Rabies has been eradicated in Britain and the rabies vaccination is usually only given to dogs in the U.K. if they will be travelling abroad.

U.S. vaccinations

Puppies receive the same vaccinations in the United States, with the exception of *Leptospirosis*, which is optional, depending on where you live.

The rabies vaccine is necessary for dogs in every state, and should be administered before the puppy is four months old.

In some areas, a vaccination for Lyme disease (spread by ticks) can also be given, but it is not considered a basic vaccination.

Some of these vaccines, such as the parvo-vaccine, need to be given more than once, over the course of several weeks. This is necessary to ensure the puppy is fully immunized.

Booster shots

Once your puppy's vaccinations are completed, he will need to have 'booster shots' at the age of one year. After that, the vaccines need to be updated every two to three years, so your puppy won't need to have all the 'jabs' done at the same time again.

List of basic dog-care accessories

a) Collar with an identity tag

b) Lead

c) Micro-chip to locate your dog if he gets lost

d) Dog-grooming items (for more information, refer to *Chapter Seven: Grooming, Cleaning & Clipping*)

e) Dog crate or pen for training and safety in the home

f) Dog-bed

g) Stainless-steel food bowl

h) Pee-pad (optional but recommended)

Feeding Bowls

Make sure your puppy can reach its food and water easily. Stainless steel bowls are best. They are more durable and easier to keep hygienic and clean.

Ceramic bowls are also a good choice, provided they are dishwasher safe. However, as soon as a ceramic bowl gets a crack in the surface, bacteria will grow there, so you should throw it out.

Plastic bowls are not a good choice, as some dogs are allergic to the material and will develop a skin reaction on the nose and muzzle. Moreover, scratches on plastic bowls also provide a good environment for bacteria to grow.

Crate

A crate is a good idea for a Lhasa Apso, not least because they are very helpful during house-training. In addition, it will keep your puppy safe when you cannot be there to watch him.

Crates are *not* puppy prisons. They are your dog's *den* and most puppies and dogs enjoy spending time in them. They also provide a safe place for dogs to relax and sleep.

Lhasa Apsos do not need a very large crate, but be sure the size of the crate will be large enough for your puppy's adult size. You can easily buy crate 'dividers' to make the crate smaller for your puppy. This will keep it the right size while your puppy is growing.

The general rule of thumb is to purchase a crate big enough to allow your fully-grown dog to stand up and turn around without a problem and to lie down comfortably.

Choosing the right crate

There are several different types of crate.

You can choose the hard-plastic crate that is used for airline travel. These crates are a good choice if you travel with your dog in your car or van, as they provide suitable protection.

Wire crates are lightweight and easy to fold up and carry. They are a good choice for people who go to shows, obedience trials and other events.

You can also buy canvas crates – though these are not recommended for dogs that like to use their claws to tear their way out of things.

Note: Never place your Lhasa inside a crate with his collar on. It is quite easy for the dog's collar to catch on the crate bars and choke the dog.

Toys

Toys are a necessity for Lhasas and for the safety of your personal items, too. When your puppy begins chewing on your favorite slippers, reach for a toy and distract your Lhasa Apso from ruining them.

If you have ever had a puppy chew your furniture, you will already know it's better to spend a little money on toys, than a lot of money repairing your living room.

Make sure you choose toys that are recommended for your dog's breed and size. Start with 'chew-toys' made especially for puppies.

Puppy teeth are sharp and they can quickly destroy toys not made for chewing and choke on the shredded pieces. Choose puppy chew toys that are made with puppy safety in mind.

Cleaning Supplies

Cleaning supplies are a necessity for homes expecting a new Lhasa puppy. Carpet and floor cleaners with special enzymes to repel dogs help to prevent further soiling. Do not forget to stock up on paper towels - you'll need them.

Dog Bed

Finally, purchase a dog bed or a crate bed for your puppy. Discourage your Lhasa Apso from jumping up onto your furniture from the start. This will help avoid 'back problems' in the future.

Even if you allow your puppy up on the furniture, it is good to have something for him to lie on in the crate. A soft faux sheepskin mat is popular with many owners and their dogs.

Or if you prefer, you can use some soft, 'fleece' blankets. 'Fleece' is warm, light and soft, making a comfortable and easy-to-wash bed for a puppy or adult dog.

Additional Supplies

The following items are optional dog accessories, which you should only buy if you feel they are necessary.

Puppy Training Pads (Pee Pads)

These are pads for your puppy to use as a toilet indoors or outdoors. The Pee Pad products have a water-proof plastic lining and a special chemical 'smell' to encourage puppies and older dogs to use them. These pads are very useful during the early stages of toilet-training.

Baby Gates

Baby gates, or pet gates, are a good way to close-off some of your rooms when your puppy comes home. Once your puppy is older and more trustworthy in the home (e.g. he won't eat the buttons off your clothes), you can put the baby gates away if you like.

Some people use them all the time to keep dogs out of certain parts of the home. For instance, you should not allow the Lhasa to be in the kitchen when you are cooking and eating meals and pet gates are handy for that.

Toys and stress reduction

In addition to the blanket that has been rubbed on the puppy's mother, toys are a very important stress reducing item for Lhasas. Look for toys that have been specially designed for use by small dogs.

Do not shower your Lhasa with lots of toys, buy two or three and when he gets bored with one toy, bring out another one. Rotating toys like this is the best way to keep them 'interesting'.

Vitamins and dietary supplements

While there can be benefits to giving an adult or senior dog vitamins or supplements, you should never do it without the advice of your vet. Some vitamins are toxic when given in high doses.

If you feed your Lhasa on a home-cooked balanced diet, it will contain a good balance of vitamins and minerals for proper growth.

Giving your puppy additional vitamins and minerals can cause musculoskeletal problems later on in life.

Puppy-proofing your home

Puppy-proofing your home is a good way to ensure you and your Lhasa Apso get off to a good start together. Otherwise she could cheerfully destroy your home while she explores it.

Here are some tips on the best ways to puppy-proof your home.

Lock away any items that can be hazardous to your Lhasa Apso, for example:

1) House-hold Cleaners

2) Vitamin pills

3) Medication

4) Car liquids such as antifreeze

5) Salts for ice or water softening

6) Pool-cleaning chemicals

7) Tobacco or e-cigarette products

Puppy's eye view

Take the time to crawl around your home before your puppy arrives and then just do a quick check once or twice a week.

Look at things from your puppy's perspective. Pick up small clips, tags, paper and anything that could be a choking hazard for her.

Do not let anyone leave their clothes on the floor. Some articles of clothing, such as socks, can pose a choking hazard for your Lhasa Apso.

Put ornaments away

Remove any ornaments that you care about until your puppy is older. Wagging tails have a way of knocking everything off a coffee table.

Puppies also like to explore by putting things in their mouths. Putting your objects away will prevent the item from being a choking hazard.

It doesn't have to be permanent, when your puppy is well-trained, you'll be able to put things back as they were.

Close-off access to standing water

Close toilet-seat lids, drain tubs and sinks and block off any access to a garden pond or pool if you have one.

Standing water can be very tempting for a Lhasa Apso.

Young puppies cannot swim well and falling into water could lead to a drowning.

Electricity cables and curtain/blind cords

Always tape up your electrical cables out of reach of your puppy, as puppies like to chew them.

Remove any cables that dangle from furniture, such as from a table-lamp. Your puppy may pull a heavy lamp down on herself while playing with the cable.

Do not forget to ensure all computer and phone cables are tucked away. Pin up any cords hanging from curtains or window-blinds. These can cause strangulation if the puppy gets caught in them.

Kitchen rubbish

Keep all kitchen waste closely covered and out of reach, or buy a puppy-proof container

Another tempting item for puppies is the dustbin. Always keep the lid closed and do not allow your puppy to sniff around the dustbin during outdoor activities.

Block-off stairs

Due to a lack of coordination, it is quite common for puppies to fall down staircases. In order to prevent this, always block off your stairs at both the top and the bottom with pet-gates.

Keep doors closed

Any door or window leading to the outside should be kept closed if the puppy can access it. An open door can be irresistible for a puppy and they can disappear in just a few seconds.

Check the outdoors

In addition to puppy-proofing your home, check your garden or yard carefully. Look for openings in the fence and garden tools that could pose a danger to your Lhasa Apso puppy.

If there are any open drains, put a tight-fitting drain-cover over them. Cover ponds and pools and remove any items that could be a danger to an inquisitive and energetic Lhasa.

Look at your plants

Finally, look at the plants you have in your home and garden. Many home-plants are poisonous to dogs, so avoid having them in your home.

If you have any poisonous plants in your garden, remove them or fence them off so your puppy cannot reach them.

Puppy-proofing is simply keeping your home neat and tidy – and taking a few extra precautions. Ask everyone in your home to pitch-in, so your puppy has a clean and safe environment to grow-up in.

Toxic Plants

Here is a list of indoor and outdoor plants that you should avoid owning alongside your Lhasa, as they are poisonous in varying degrees.

Aconite	Emerald Feather	Nightshade
Aloe Vera	English Ivy	Oaks
Amaryllis	Eucalyptus	Oleander
Apple Leaf Croton	European Bittersweet	Onions
Arrow grasses	False Flax	Oriental Lily
Asparagus Fern	False Hellebore	Peace Lily
Atropa belladonna	Fan Weed	Peach Tree
Autumn Crocus	Fiddle-leaf Fig	Pencil Cactus
Azalea	Field Peppergrass	Philodendrons
Baby's Breath	Florida Beauty	Plumosa Fern
Baneberry	Foxglove	Pokeweed
Bird of Paradise	Fruit Salad Plant	Poinsettia
Black Locust	Geranium	Poison Hemlock

Bloodroot	German Ivy	Poison Ivy
Box	Giant Dumb Cane	Poison Oak
Branching Ivy	Glacier Ivy	Potato Plant
Buckeye	Gold Dust Dracaena	Pothos
Buddhist Pine	Golden Pothos	Precatory Bean
Buttercup	Hahn's Self-Branching Ivy	Primrose
Caladium	Heartland Philodendron	Rattle box
Calla Lily	Holly	Red Emerald
Carolina Jessamine	Horse Chestnut	Red Princess
Castor Bean	Horse Nettle	Red-Margined Dracaena
Ceriman	Hurricane Plant	Rhododendron
Charming Dieffenbachia	Indian Rubber Plant	Rhubarb
Cherry Tree	Iris	Ribbon Plant
Chinaberry Tree	Jack-in-the-Pulpit	Rosary Pea
Chinese Evergreen	Japanese Show Lily	Saddle Leaf Philodendron
Chock Cherries	Jatropha	Sago Palm
Christmas Berry	Jerusalem Cherry	Satin Pothos
Christmas Rose	Jimsonweed	Schefflera
Cineraria	Kalan Choe	Skunk Cabbage
Clematis	Labarum	Silver Pothos
Common Privet	Lacey Tree Philodendron	Smartweeds
Cordatum	Lantana	Snow-on-the-Mountain
Corn Cockle	Laurels	Sorghum
Corn Plant	Lily of the Valley	Spotted Dumb Cane
Cornstalk Plant	Lupines	Star of Bethlehem
Cowbane	Madagascar Dragon Tree	String of Pearls
Cow Cockle	Manchineel Tree	Striped Dracaena
Cowslip	Marble Queen	Sweetheart Ivy

Croton	Marijuana	Swiss Cheese Plant
Cuban Laurel	Matrimony Vine	Taro Vine
Cutleaf Philodendron	May Apple	Tiger Lily
Cycads	Mexican Breadfruit	Tomato Plant
Cyclamen	Milk Vetch	Tree Philodendron
Daffodil	Miniature Croton	Tropic Snow Dieffenbachia
Daphne	Mistletoe	Velvet Grass
Death Camas	Monk's Hood	Weeping Fig
Delphinium	Moonseed	Wild Black Cherry
Devil's Ivy	Morning Glory	Wild Radish
Dieffenbachia,	Mother-in Law's Tongue	Wisteria
Dracaena Palm	Mountain Mahogany	Wood Aster
Dragon Tree	Mustards	Yellow Jessamine
Dumb Cane	Narcissus	Yellow Oleander
Dutchman's Breeches	Needlepoint Ivy	Yellow Pine Flax
Elephant Ears	Nephthytis	Yew

Chapter Five: Bringing your New Puppy Home

The day you pick up your Lhasa Apso puppy is always exciting, especially if you have had a long wait to obtain her.

It can be difficult to stay calm, but it is important to do so for the sake of your puppy. She will be nervous and frightened during this huge change. When you are calm, it is reassuring to your puppy.

To make the transition go smoothly, send a blanket to the breeder a few days before-hand and ask her to rub it on the puppy's siblings and mother.

If that is not possible, take a blanket with you when you collect your puppy. Rub your natural sweat smell on it and at the kennels, rub that blanket on the mother and siblings. This will help your puppy to associate you with the comforting smells of her family.

Leave the children at home

It is usually best to leave your children at home when you pick up a new Lhasa Apso puppy. This is true whether you are picking the puppy up at the breeder's home or going to the airport.

Moving to a new home is a stressful time for a Lhasa Apso and the excitement of children can greatly increase his anxiety.

Before you leave home, have everything set up so you can simply place him in his 'safe place', in the dog-pen with the comfort-blanket.

Airport pick-up

In some cases, you may be picking-up a puppy at the airport, especially if you have found a breeder that lives a long distance from you.

If this is the case, then you and the breeder should discuss everything over the phone before-hand in detail.

Puppies travelling by air must have all of the available health certificates and vaccination records, as well as other travel papers.

Ensure the breeder sends you the puppy's travel information in good time, so you know where and when the puppy is arriving.

Different airlines handle shipping dogs in different ways, so it is a good idea to call the airline in advance and make sure you have all the correct details.

Fresh water and toilet break

Dogs can and do get lost at airports, so resist the temptation to open your puppy's crate as soon as you see him. Wait until you have the crate safely secured in your vehicle before you open the door.

Give him some fresh water to drink and then put on the collar and lead. Next, visit a suitable rest area where your puppy can relieve himself and offer him some more fresh water.

Try to plan ahead, so you can stop at a secluded spot and avoid contact with other dogs. This is to prevent infection from dogs which may not have been vaccinated and may be carriers of disease.

Let your puppy eliminate and then pick him up immediately and put him back into his travel-crate.

Car-safety

Puppies should never sit on the driver's lap or be loose in the car, where they are bound to distract the driver and make safe driving impossible. If you are collecting your puppy from the breeder's home, always use a travel-crate.

Once you arrive at the breeder's home, spend some time with your puppy, his littermates, his mother, and with the breeder. If you have some last minute questions, try to have them written down in advance, so you won't forget them.

Building a good relationship with your puppy's breeder is important. She will be a valuable source of advice and guidance throughout your puppy's life.

On the way home

After you leave the breeder's home, or collect your puppy from an airport, where possible, try to go straight home.

Do not stop to visit a friend or go to a pet store. At this age, your puppy is very susceptible to disease and stop-offs will expose him to danger and cause extra stress.

Try to keep your puppy calm and do not worry about showing him off just yet, your puppy will soon be able to go out and visit friends with you.

Car-sickness

Keep an eye on your Lhasa Apso puppy in the car. Many puppies experience motion sickness in cars. It is possible that your puppy has already taken some car trips to the vet, but some puppies experience car-sickness.

It is a good idea to cover your car upholstery with a large plastic sheet. Then you can just gather it up later and dispose of it. Or take some paper towels and cleaner with you.

Vomiting

If you see your puppy's nose drooping towards the floor, with drooling and wrinkling of the lips, he's preparing to vomit. This is perfectly normal, so be prepared to stop the car and allow him time to get over his car-sickness.

Crating your puppy during car rides is safer for the puppy and cleaner if he vomits. Cleaning a crate is easier than having to clean the upholstery and carpet.

At home for the first time

When you get home, take your puppy outside immediately to relieve himself in the area chosen by you. (for more information, refer to *Chapter Eight: Socialization & House-Training*)

Puppies will usually sniff the chosen area, (so give praise, strokes and gentle pats for this), and then relieve themselves.

Once your puppy has finished, take him inside the home and go to a quiet room together. Sit with your Lhasa Apso puppy and let him explore his new surroundings.

Some Lhasa Apso puppies will want to play and run around, others will want to sleep in their dog-pen. Follow your puppy's cues.

Keep your puppy confined to one area at first. Then slowly open up your home as he becomes more confident and trustworthy in terms of house-training.

The key to introducing your puppy to his new home successfully, is being calm, progressing slowly and creating rules and schedules to make him feel secure.

Introducing your Lhasa Apso to family and friends

Introduce your puppy to family members slowly. Keep all interactions with the new puppy calm. During the first few days you will find your Lhasa Apso sleeps a lot.

This is normal for all puppies at a young age. However, this will change as he becomes familiar with his home and as he gets older and gains confidence.

As far as home rules are concerned, keep to a schedule for house-training and stick to your rules. A schedule will help your puppy know when and where he is supposed to potty.

Take it slowly

While your first instinct is probably to rush on and introduce him to everyone you know, take note that your Lhasa Apso can become very frightened by too much attention all at once.

A puppy can withdraw and 'shut down' when overwhelmed by new surroundings or too many people. Since you want all introductions to be positive, make the introductions as calmly as possible.

After allowing your puppy to rest in a quiet room, begin taking your fellow residents into the room to meet him – one at a time.

Other animals in the home can wait a day or two. There is no rush and if you do the introductions properly, this will prevent any lasting problems for your Lhasa Apso.

Children and Lhasa Apsos

Lhasa Apsos are not recommended for homes with young children. However, in circumstances where you cannot avoid them being together, here is how to keep both parties safe.

For younger children, it is a good idea to introduce them to your Lhasa Apso puppy one at a time. This will help minimize the amount of stimulation the puppy has. If you have older children, you can introduce them together.

When you are introducing your Lhasa Apso puppy to children, start by having your child come into the room and sit down on the floor. Do not rush the puppy or place the puppy in your child's lap.

Instead, give your child treats to feed the puppy and allow the puppy to approach on his own terms. Tell the child to stay calm and quiet so the puppy won't get frightened.

When the puppy does greet the child, let the child pet the Lhasa Apso calmly.

Always supervise

Keep meetings short and build up their length over the first few days. Supervise all interactions with the children to maintain a calm and quiet atmosphere.

As the puppy gets used to the sounds of children, you can start introducing play times.

It is important that children should have rules regarding the puppy and they should be taught how to treat the dog. Make sure your children understand the following rules:

1) Be calm around the puppy

2) Don't hold onto him when he wants to go

3) Never hit or pinch the puppy

4) Do not pull on ears or tail

5) Gently pet the puppy

6) Use toys to play with the puppy

7) Do not try to take toys or food away from a puppy or dog

8) Do not run away from a puppy or dog

Puppies do not respect small children

Most puppies and dogs do not respect children in the same way they do the adult (taller) members of the family. Your children won't be able to cue your puppy with the same authority that you have until they are a little older.

It is important that an adult is *always* present to supervise small children playing with, or near to, puppies and dogs to keep accidents from happening. Once your children are a little older, your dog will respect them more and play is less likely to get out of hand.

As you train your Lhasa Apso puppy, you should include your children in the puppy's training and socialization. This will be helpful for both your puppy and your children in the long run.

Do Lhasa Apsos get along with other pets?

Your Lhasa might be small and sweet, but he is also brave and dominant by nature. For that reason, he is often not a friendly dog towards other pets in your home.

How to socialize your Lhasa Apso with other pets

Introducing your Lhasa Apso puppy to other pets in the home is something you should do gradually. Remember that animals already in the home were there first and may well exhibit behavioral problems owing to jealousy or problems with territory.

Moreover, if you already have other dogs, or dogs that visit your home frequently, take every dog's personality into consideration. Everything will depend on whether the, 'other', dog is dominant or submissive – because Lhasas like to be the dominant dog.

Short and sweet

To prevent problems, ensure that the first meetings are short and do not force any relationships. The animals in your home will sort out their hierarchy on their own, but be prepared for your Lhasa Apso wanting to be the head of the pack, second only to you.

Here are some useful guidelines for pet meetings:

1. Keep your puppy confined

The first rule is that you should always keep your puppy confined when you take him home. Place your Lhasa Apso in a quiet room.

This will keep your new puppy safe and your current pet will not feel directly challenged.

When you are taking the puppy out of his room, always confine the current dog - unless you are taking the time to introduce them.

2. Allow door sniffing

Door sniffing and crate sniffing are important to your puppy, so always allow him time to do this. In addition, you should allow your current pet to sniff at the crate or the door where the puppy is.

a) This will help your pet become acquainted with the puppy, with a *safe* barrier between pet and puppy.

b) Do not let them be pushy during initial meetings and if your puppy starts to look stressed, stop the interaction straight away.

Setting up a meeting with current pet dog

1) Plan the meetings between your current pet and the Lhasa puppy in advance.

2) Never take a puppy into the room where your current pet is and allow the older dog to take charge.

3) Wait until your current pet is calm before you make the introductions. This will help promote a positive experience for both your new Lhasa Apso and your current pet.

4) Encourage your current pet to equate your puppy with positives When you are doing the introductions, always provide the older dog with plenty of affection.

5) Give lots of praise and physical strokes/pats for greeting nicely and make sure you give him plenty of treats.

The more you praise your current pet, the more he will think the new Lhasa Apso puppy is something positive.

Cats

While you can control the meetings between a dog and puppy, it can be difficult to control the meeting between a Lhasa puppy and cat.

Puppies often find cats interesting (*too interesting sometimes*) and will try to chase the cat or play with it. When this happens, the cat will feel threatened and can react aggressively.

1) The best approach is to let the cat watch the Lhasa puppy from its own vantage points.

2) Praise, treat, and pet the cat when you are able to do so, to keep it feeling comfortable with the new excitement in the home.

3) After a few weeks, start taking your cat down from its *perches,* to be nearer to the young Lhasa, but only when the puppy is calm.

4) Do not introduce the cat in the middle of a boisterous play session.

5) Always make sure you have full control of your Lhasa Apso puppy, to prevent him chasing the cat.

It may take time, but eventually your Lhasa Apso will make friends with the cat, though it will always be on the cat's terms.

Make the older pet the primary pet

What this means is that your current pet should have more rights than the puppy.

The current pet should be fed first, you should greet him first when you get home, and you should always allow the current pet to enter or exit first.

It may be hard to believe, but if you support your older pet's position, it shows the puppy that he must respect the older pet.

Rights of seniority

You will avoid fights over status and rank if you support your older pet's rights. Your puppy may try to challenge your older pet's authority, but it is up to you to promote your older pet if you want peace in your home.

As the animals become used to each other, you can start offering more attention and other things *equally*, but for the first few months, make the current pet feel extra-special.

Occasionally, an older dog may be happy to allow a Lhasa puppy to assume leadership and that always works out very well.

Be patient

Finally, be patient with your pets. Remember that this is a huge change of environment and companions for them. It can take up to 6 months for the puppy to be accepted by the current pets.

Chapter Six: Food and Dog Health

The older generation of vets have often written about the noticeable decline in the health of dogs during their life-time.

From the 1950's in the U.S. and the 1970's and 80's in Britain, convenience food for dogs has been advertised as healthy food. However, it is not healthy food and often contains high quantities of corn and other bulking agents, which are not good for dogs.

Remember that the expensive advertisements presenting dog-foods as, 'perfectly balanced nutrition', or, 'luxury food', are *not* necessarily true.

Commercial dog-foods are almost exclusively made with meat that has been 'condemned' by the meat inspector. This means the meat has been marked as *unfit for human consumption* because it has 'gone off', comes from diseased animals, or is in some other way unusable.

Avoid corn additives

Cereals like corn-starch and corn-oil in particular are used to bulk out dog-foods, along with lots of extra fat and artificial colors and 'flavorings'. These unhealthy additives often cause illness in pets.

Every day, vets treat the unnecessary ailments that commercial dog foods cause. These include:

1) Diarrhea

2) Excessive itchiness (hot spots) caused by food-allergies

3) Face-rubbing

4) Foot-licking

5) Hair-loss

6) Severe dandruff

7) Upset stomach and passing foul-smelling gas

8) Bladder and kidney stones

Not to mention the more severe conditions that can cause the early death of a beloved Lhasa Apso companion.

Dry-foods

The cheapest food that you can give a dog is dry-food. Dry-food is full of carbohydrate fillers such as corn. It is popular as a cheap (but unhealthy) way to feed large dogs and includes pellets, flaked food, mixes, biscuits and kibbles.

You can give your Lhasa dry food occasionally, but mash it up with water if possible and leave fresh water available.

Are carbohydrates needed in a Lhasas diet?

Many animal nutritionists believe Lhasas should not be fed any carbohydrates. Dr. D. S. Kronfeld says that adult dogs – even working dogs - do not need carbohydrates.

This is because their liver makes enough glucose from a diet of meat protein and fats.

This underlines the advice to avoid feeding your Lhasa any commercial foods containing bulking-up additives, like yellow sweet corn, beetroot pulp or potatoes.

Yellow sweet corn cannot even be *digested* by a dog, showing that corn has no nutritional value to your pet.

Other proof of this belief is that humans – who are omnivores or vegetarians - have *amylase* in their saliva. *Amylase* is a substance that helps humans digest carbohydrates in food.

On the other hand, carnivores such as dogs and cats, which have evolved primarily as 'meat-eaters', do not have *amylase* in their saliva. This means that if you feed them carbohydrate foods, they cannot digest them. This can cause health problems in dogs/cats.

Fresh meat

Dogs are carnivores. They need a diet of fresh, or frozen-while-fresh, meat to be healthy.

Commercial canned meats are cooked at incredibly high temperatures, in an effort to kill-off the worst bacteria in the 'condemned meat' they use. This removes the essential enzymes and anti-oxidants your dog needs.

Even if the canning factory started off with prime cuts of beef, after this heat-processing it would be heavily lacking in nutrition.

Omega oils

Lhasas also need Omega 3 and Omega 6 oils, from eating fish like tinned sardines in oil.

The 'Omega-oils' advertised in processed dog-food lose their benefit after being over-processed. They often end up turning rancid, too, after being stored for extended periods.

Best foods for the Lhasa Apso

Good dog food always has meat as the main ingredient. Along with muscle-meat, like ground beef and chicken breast, it should also contain: heart, liver, kidney, bone or bone meal.

There are several different views about the correct diet for Lhasa Apsos. One is the raw food diet championed by Dr. Ian Billinghurst.

1. Raw diet

If you opt for the raw diet, recommended by many Lhasa Apso owners and vets, here's a sample of a typical diet. This would become the diet for life for a fully-grown dog.

a) Finely mashed-up ground beef for puppies

b) From 8 weeks of age, add raw minced lamb and beef plus raw eggs three times a week and sardines in oil once a week

c) Around 14 weeks of age add minced chicken

d) Either goat's milk (the nearest you can get to Lhasa Apso mother's milk)

e) Or lactose-free milk up to 6 months

f) Or a calcium supplement for dogs

What about the risk of salmonella?

Yes, that is the problem with only feeding your pet on raw food. There is always a risk of raw meat or eggs containing salmonella, E.coli and other toxic bacteria. These can cause fatal illness in humans and dogs.

2. Home-cooked diet

Therefore, the home-cooked mainly meat diet - with fish - is one that many owners would recommend.

Lightly-cooked, fresh or frozen meats will retain the essential enzymes and anti-oxidants needed to keep your pet healthy and disease-free.

You can use shop-bought frozen meat to cook and keep in the fridge for a day or two.

Or buy fresh meat, which you can cook-up in a batch of meat-stew and then freeze in handy meal-size portions for convenience.

Breeder's dietary advice is vital

If you want a healthy dog that lives its full life-span, you should *only* take advice on your Lhasa's diet from:

1) An experienced and affiliated Lhasa breeder.

2) An experienced vet who has studied the Lhasa Apso breed and understands their nutritional needs.

Other suitable foods for Lhasa Apsos

a) Cottage cheese (but not cow's milk or other types of cheese)

b) Lightly scrambled eggs

c) Oats as cooked porridge

What not to feed your Lhasa Apso dog

a) No cow's milk

b) No 'human food' from the dinner-table

c) No onions (contain thiosulphate, which is toxic to dogs)

d) No chocolate (contains theobromine which is toxic to dogs)

e) Nothing with 'corn' in *any* form, listed in the ingredients

f) Nothing containing artificial colors, flavors or other chemical additives

The full list of foods that you should never give to your dog can be found later in this chapter, under the ***Foods to Avoid*** section.

Vitamins and Supplements

If you make your dog's food at home, you will know you are providing a fully balanced diet containing essential vitamins and minerals for the breed.

Never give your Lhasa any extra vitamins or food supplements without consulting your vet first. What is good for humans can be poisonous for dogs.

Avoid Vitamin C supplements

In particular, do not give your Lhasa Apso any vitamin C supplements, as they damage the liver and kidneys of this breed. These are often listed on pill bottles or packs as:

a) Ascorbic acid

b) Sodium ascorbate

c) Calcium ascorbate

d) Ascorbal palmitate

Avoiding digestion problems

In the early days, you will need to follow the same diet as has been used at the breeder's home.

Whenever you change food for a puppy or an adult dog, make the change slowly over several days to avoid a stomach upset.

Save money

It is much cheaper in the long-term to feed your Lhasa Apso on home-cooked food recommended by your puppy's breeder.

No-one want wants to pay high vets' fees, caused by feeding their valuable pedigree dog a mainly kibble and commercial dog-food diet.

How often to feed puppies and adults

You should feed a puppy three times per day: once in the morning, once around lunch time and once in the evening.

As your puppy grows, you can begin to leave out the lunch feeding and move to two meals a day. Never feed only one meal a day, as this can cause stomach problems for your dog.

If you stick to a fixed schedule of feeding, your dog will also have a regular time for needing the toilet. This makes life a lot easier for owners and more comfortable for your pet.

Feeding methods

Lhasa's can sometimes be 'fussy eaters', but I would advise against leaving food out all day. If there are other pets in the house, they will probably try eating your Lhasa's food.

This may provoke *food-protection aggression* and even fighting between your pets. If you have ever had small children you will know *exactly* what that's like.

Put the food down and walk away, as dogs like to be left alone when they are eating. Leave each meal out for about 20 minutes and then remove it.

If your dog has not eaten all of a meal, put it in the fridge inside a clean plastic bag and then make it part of the next scheduled feed. Your Lhasa will soon realize that she should eat-up within the 20 minute 'meal-time'.

This is the best way to keep your dog fit, because you can control how much she is eating. If she misses more than one meal because of lack of appetite, contact your vet.

Providing snacks and treats

Treats can be an important tool for training your pet's behavior as well as building up your relationship bond. In the wild, pack leaders' control the eating hierarchy. Therefore, receiving tiny, but tasty treats from your hand will back up your authority.

To avoid over-feeding and the many illnesses related to over-weight in dogs, only use treats as a training reward. Do not feed your pet any human foods as treats *ever*. This can cause a wide range of health problems from painful stomach upsets to quite serious illness.

Low-calorie, home-made healthy treats based on a sliver of dried tuna or salmon are the best, because they are tasty and will not cause weight gain. It is quite easy to dry bits of fish in the oven, when you are cooking family meals.

Here is a list of healthy snack choices for your Lhasa Apso:

Apples (remove seeds)	Kale
Applesauce	Lemons
Apricots (remove pits)	Marrow Bones (raw only)
Baby food (all-natural, make sure it is free of salt)	Mint
Bananas	Nectarines (remove pits)
Beef (raw and cooked)	Oatmeal
Beets	Organ meats (heart, liver, kidney, etc.)
Blackberries	Pasta (cooked)
Blueberries	Peaches (remove pits)
Bran cereal	Peanut butter
Bread (avoid nut breads and raison bread)	Pears
Broccoli (safe when fed raw)	Peas
Brussels Sprouts	Pineapple
Cantaloupe	Plums (remove pits)
Carrots	Pumpkin
Cauliflower: safe when fed raw	Rice: cooked only
Celery	Rice cakes
Cheerios cereal	Salmon
Cheese (cheddar is safe)	Spinach
Chicken (remove bones if cooked)	Squash
Corn: safe off the cob	Strawberries
Cottage cheese	Sweet potatoes

Cranberries	Tomatoes
Cream cheese	Training treats
Cucumbers	Tuna
Dog Cookies (homemade and store bought)	Turkey (cooked without bones)
Eggs (when cooked)	Watermelon
Flax seed	Yogurt
Green beans	Zucchini
Honey	

How much to feed

Feeding differs depending on the age of your dog, how active the dog is and the type of food you are feeding. High quality dog foods require less food while low quality foods require more, so your dog can reach the necessary caloric intake. With feeding, it is important to look at the weight of your dog, as well as his energy level and age.

To do this, we have to look at the resting energy requirements. What this means is that when your dog is resting, how many calories is he burning? From there, we can begin to adjust the amount of food, or calories that we need to feed the dog.

Determining your dog's resting energy requirements (RER) formula is simple.

RER in kcal/day = 30 (body weight in kilograms) + 70

Take your dog's weight in kilograms and multiply it by 30. Then add 70. This can also work if you are using pounds but just be sure to convert the weight into kilograms first.

For example, if you have a 13 pound Lhasa Apso, you would divide 13 by 2.2 for a total of 5.91 or 6 kilograms, if we round up. Then, multiply 6 by 30 for 180 and then add 70 for a total of 250 calories per day. Most dog food bags have the calorie amount for every half cup or cup so you simply divide the calories needed by the calories provided and spread them over the number of meals you are feeding.

For instance, Purina Dog Chow Complete Nutrition has 430 calories for every cup of dog food. So dividing 430 into 250 means that the dog would need slightly more than 1/2 cups of food to meet his caloric intake needs. This is the resting energy requirement for a dog, but they can have a variety of situations.

For example, a dog might be pregnant or neutered or have light activity. You can check the chart below to find the number to multiply by your dog's resting energy requirement.

Activity Level/Age	Multiplier for Resting Energy Requirements
Weaning to 4 months	X 3.0
4 months to adult	X 2.0
Lactating female	X 4.8
Pregnant female day 1 to 42	X 1.8
Pregnant female day 42 to whelping	X 3.0
Adult Dog neutered/spayed with normal activity	X 1.6
Adult Dog intact with normal activity	X 1.8
Adult Dog with light activity	X 2.0
Adult Dog with moderate activity	X 3.0
Adult Dog with heavy activity	X 4.8
Adult Dog needing weight loss	X 1.0

As you can see, the daily calories can change depending on the individual dog. So if the same Lhasa Apso from above, that needs 250 calories per day, was a lactating female that was nursing puppies, her calories for the day should be 1200 or 2 ¾ cups of Purina Dog Chow.

Fortunately, most dog food companies have already done this math for you. The guidelines that they include on their labels are based on these figures so you can use their suggestions for how much to feed your dog as a starting point. You will need to watch your puppy or dog when you start feeding him a dog food, to see if he is gaining or losing weight and his overall condition. You can make adjustments to his portions accordingly.

When we are looking at RAW feeding, the amounts are slightly different. In addition, it is difficult to determine the calories as it will be different with the food you are giving. A pound of beef with 30% blend of organ, meat and bone has about 2600 calories in it, so the Lhasa Apso that weighs 13 pounds only needs about 0.1 pounds of food per day. The reason for this is because the multiplier for the resting energy requirements is higher when feeding raw, which is outlined in the chart on the next page.

Activity Level/Age	Multiplier for Resting Energy Requirements
Weaning to 4 months	X 6.0
4 months to adult	X 4.0
Lactating female	X 8.0
Pregnant female day 1 to 42	X 4.0
Pregnant female day 42 to whelping	X 6.0
Adult Dog neutered/spayed with normal activity	X 2.0
Adult Dog intact with normal activity	X 2.5
Adult Dog with light activity	X 3.0
Adult Dog with moderate activity	X 3.5
Adult Dog with heavy activity	X 4.0
Adult Dog needing weight loss	X 1.5

Adult dogs

With adult or housetrained dogs, you can leave the water down all the time.

To check if your dog has drunk enough water each day, the rule is 1 ounce (oz.) of water for every pound (lb.) of weight or 66 ml. for every kilogram of dog.

Providing water at the optimal time

Generally speaking, young puppies that are not fully house-trained should only be offered water at set times. This will help reduce the number of times they need to go to the bathroom.

Another good rule with young dogs is to pick up the water dish about 2 hours before you go to bed. This will help your puppy make it comfortably through the night without a full bladder.

Foods to Avoid

Here are some foods that you should never feed your dog. While some foods are safe for people, there are a range of foods that can have catastrophic effects on your Lhasa Apso if you feed them to him.

Below is a table that goes over foods you should avoid giving to your dog.

Foods to Avoid	Reasons to Avoid
Alcohol	Can lead to a coma and/or death
Apple Seeds	Seeds contain cyanide and can lead to death.
Artificial Sweetener	Can cause low blood sugar, vomiting, collapse and liver failure.
Avocado	May cause vomiting and diarrhea
Broccoli	When cooked, it can cause gas, which can lead to bloating. Safe when it is raw.
Cat Food	While not harmful, too much cat food can lead to health problems due to the high protein and fat content.
Cauliflower	When cooked, it can cause gas, which can lead to bloating. Safe when it is raw.
Chocolate	Contains caffeine and theobromine and can lead to vomiting and diarrhea. Can lead to death if too much is consumed.
Cooked Chicken Bones	Cooked chicken has bones that can splinter, which can lead to an obstruction or laceration in the digestive system.
Citrus Oil	May cause vomiting.

Coffee	Contains caffeine and can lead to vomiting and diarrhea. Can lead to death if too much is consumed.
Currants	Can cause kidney damage and death.
Fat Trimmings	High fat levels can lead to pancreatitis.
Any fish that has not been de-boned or Bone-in Fish	Bones can lacerate the digestive system. In addition, if fed a fish exclusive diet, it can lead to vitamin B deficiency, which can cause seizures and death. Fish in dog food is fine as long as other nutrients are in the ingredients list. Fish skin is also a nutritious treat.
Garlic	In large doses, can cause anemia.
Grapes	Can cause kidney damage and death.
Grape Seed Oil	Can cause kidney damage and death.
Gum	Can cause blockages and contains Xylitol, which can damage the liver.
Hops	Can cause increased heart rate, fever, seizures and sometimes, death.
Human Vitamins	Can damage a dog's liver, kidneys and digestive system.
Macadamia Nuts	Toxin in the nuts can cause seizures and death.
Milk	Along with other dairy products, can cause diarrhea.
Mushrooms	Can cause shock, shut down multiple body systems and can lead to death.
Onions	Can cause anemia.
Persimmons	The seeds lead to intestinal obstructions.
Peaches	The flesh of the peach is fine, but be sure to remove the pit or it can cause an obstruction.

Pork	Contains bones that will splinter, which can lead to an obstruction or laceration in the digestive system.
Plum Pits	The flesh of the plum is fine, but be sure to remove the pit or it can cause an obstruction.
Raisins	Can cause kidney damage and death.
Raw Eggs	Can cause skin and coat problems since it decreases the absorption of biotin.
Rhubarb Leaves	Poisonous, can affect the urinary tract system, digestive system and nervous system.
Salt	Can lead to vomiting, diarrhea, dehydration and seizures. Large quantities can lead to death.
Sugar	Leads to obesity and has been linked to canine diabetes.
Tea	Contains caffeine and can lead to vomiting and diarrhea. Can lead to death if too much is consumed.
Tomato Greens/Plant	Can cause heart problems in dogs.
Turkey	Cooked turkey has bones that will splinter, which can lead to an obstruction or laceration in the digestive system.
Yeast	Can cause pain, gas and can even cause a rupture in the digestive system, which can result in death.

Chapter Seven: Grooming, Cleaning & Clipping

Grooming is an important part of caring for a Lhasa Apso. You need to do a little daily grooming yourself to ensure their lovely coat does not become tangled or matted.

If you will not have the time to groom your Lhasa regularly, have her coat clipped short. Then you and your dog will both be happy.

You will need to find a good Lhasa Apso grooming salon, to have your dog's hair cleaned, trimmed and maintained at the length you prefer.

Actually, very few dog groomers know how to groom Lhasa Apsos correctly, so here is a handy list of questions to ask – just to check they really *do* know what needs to be done.

Questions to ask potential Lhasa Apso groomers

1) Do you know how to do a scissor cut?

2) How do you clean and groom the ears?

3) How do you prevent cross-infection when cleaning ears?

4) Do you include cleaning the anal glands?

5) What do you class as a puppy coat?

6) What do you do with the paws?

7) What brand of products do you use?

8) Do you have experience with untangling a matted long coat on an Apso – can you show me what you normally do?

9) How do you deal with the facial hair?

10) Do you mind if I stay and watch how you bathe and groom my dog?

I would recommend to every Lhasa Apso dog-owner that, at least for the first session with a new groomer, you stay and observe. Grooming services are not cheap and you should make sure *they* know that *you* expect the best treatment for your valued pet.

Beware untrained groomers

While many of us would rather leave quietly than tell a hairdresser she's made a mess of our *own* hair, do not be shy about refusing to pay any grooming bill that has not followed your instructions.

During my experience with Lhasas, I have heard some incredible stories about over-confident/incompetent groomers. Some groomers ruin the little dogs' coat and then hold out their hand for payment – so do not trust anyone.

Home grooming and clipping

Lots of Lhasa owners find that learning how to groom their pet at home is a very rewarding and pleasant experience.

It is not something you can learn overnight – but dog-bathing and grooming sessions can be a lovely way of sharing closeness and affection with your pet.

Lots of owners find it very relaxing, too.

Tools for Lhasa Apso grooming

You really do not need to buy lots of special gadgets to put together a full Lhasa Apso grooming kit. Here is a list of what you need:

1) A normal dog-grooming pin brush

2) An extra-soft smoothing brush

3) A wide-toothed metal comb

4) A narrow-toothed metal comb

5) Dog toe-nail clippers

6) A plastic spray bottle of coat conditioning oil or anti-static de-tangler diluted in water

7) A pair of sharp scissors

8) Some broad elastic bands

9) A hair dryer

Training your puppy to accept regular grooming

From an early age, train your puppy to lie on her back and on her side and allow you to groom her coat.

The time to do this is when your pet has had her exercise for the day and is tired, so she is comfortable lying quietly.

Lhasa Apso puppies do not actually need much grooming, as their coat is not fully grown. However, training them from a young age to co-operate with grooming sessions will pay huge dividends later on.

How to brush Lhasa Apso hair correctly

With your dog settled on her back or side, gently push the coat against its natural growing direction to expose the undercoat and start by grooming the stomach.

Starting from the lowest layers, spray a fine mist of diluted anti-static de-tangler or crème rinse on one layer at a time and then brush it through, gently but firmly.

Your general direction should be from the bottom layers to the top, turning your pet over to repeat the grooming on the other side, in this order:

1) Stomach

2) Inside front legs

3) Inside back legs

4) Outside front legs

5) Outside back legs

6) Chest, neck and ears – including behind the ears

7) Finishing with the crown of the head and face

How to remove matted sections of Lhasa Apso hair

Lightly matted hair just needs a good spray of coat conditioning oil or de-tangler to lubricate it.

Leave it for a minute to penetrate and then gently untangle it with your fingers and finish off with a comb through - from the tips to the roots.

If the section is badly matted and solid, spray the whole tangled area with coat conditioning oil (or de-tangler) until it is saturated and follow these guidelines:

1) Use your fingers to work the oil into the tightly packed hair gently.

2) Then leave it for a minute or two, to warm up and penetrate the matted section further.

3) Then, with a lot of patience, begin to ease the matted hairs apart with your fingers. First of all, you will just have two matted lumps and then four and so on, until you have done as much as you can with your fingers.

4) As you make progress towards the center of the knots, spray a little more oil onto the tangles to lubricate the hairs and make them slippery enough to slide out.

5) Next, you can use the end tooth of your dog-comb to loosen the smaller clumps. Always start combing from the bottom-ends of the hair first, and move up towards the roots.

6) Never place the comb in a section above a tangle and try to force it down the hair-shafts, as you will cause pain to your dog and just make the knot tighter or rip out a large chunk of your

dog's coat.

7) If you are not able to reduce the original matted area enough to follow this method, and are faced with a solidly packed 'lump', you may have to resort to using the scissors to cut it out.

Bathing your Lhasa Apso

Should you de-tangle before or after bathing?

It has been found that a good brush through *before* the bath is essential, as it avoids the hairs swelling-up with water.

Tangles that are soaked with warm water swell and become tight knots. In addition, matted areas will become very heavy and impossible to brush or comb out.

However, if you groom your Lhasa Apso every day and keep her coat completely tangle-free, you can certainly bathe first and de-tangle later.

Bathing technique – How to avoid tangling your Lhasas hair

In order to avoid tangling your Lhasa's coat during the washing, do not rub shampoo into the hairs in a circular motion. This will create more knots than you ever want to see on your pet.

1. Wet your dog completely and then apply the shampoo moving from the *roots to the tips* – so you are smoothing the hair cuticles down in their natural direction as you go.

2. Use a 'squeezing' motion to help the shampoo penetrate the dog's thick coat as you move down the sections of hair.

3. You will still get soap-suds this way, although you do not need soapy foam to clean a dog's coat.

4. Be gentle, but firm, and keep resisting the urge to rub circles

until the entire coat has been shampooed.

5. After rinsing, again from root to tip, use your hands to squeeze the excess water from the ears, legs and tail and lift your Lhasa out of the bath or shower cubicle.

Drying the coat

1. Do not undo all of your good work by rubbing your pet briskly all over with a towel.

2. Use a dry towel *to blot* the dog's coat to remove the water and move from *root to tip*.

3. Then use a second dry towel *to squeeze* the sections of hair gently, until the coat is ready to be blown dry with a hair-dryer.

4. Lastly, lay your dog on its side and start brushing out the layers from bottom to top.

5. Then blow each layer dry with a hair-drier carefully set at a *low - medium* temperature and speed.

6. Remember not to place the drier too close to your pet's skin or it may feel too hot. Lhasa's usually love this part of the grooming process.

7. Pay special attention to the inside of the legs and behind the ears to ensure your dog will be completely dry.

Flea treatment for Lhasa Apsos

A good time to check your dog's skin for flea bites or skin mites is while you are drying her coat after bathing.

The best way to avoid or treat fleas is to use a good quality flea treatment and apply it regularly.

If you notice your dog is itching all the time, I would recommend you take her to the vet for a proper examination.

There are several skin problems that cause severe itching and until you have a diagnosis, you won't know the correct treatment.

If your dog is allergic to flea-bites, you will need to stay on top of her skin care.

Some dogs have skin-mites, which are not visible to the naked eye. They cause terrible itchiness on your dog's skin.

Skin-mites can be treated by dipping your dog in a special, medicated solution recommended by your vet.

Choosing flea treatments

Some of the flea treatments in shops are better than others and you may have to try more than one to get the best treatment for your particular dog.

Products such as, *Revolution*, will worm your dog, (except for tape-worms), and provides heartworm protection, too. It also protects against fleas, ticks, ear mites and two types of mange.

Frontline is another well reviewed flea prevention product. However, some owners say it only works for a few days, instead of a full month.

Comfortis® is a chewable, beef-flavored tablet that the manufacturer claims will start killing fleas within 30 minutes and prevent fleas for 30 days.

Available in the U.S., *Comfortis*® is advertised as the first FDA-approved, chewable flea-killing tablet.

However, some of the side-effects of *chemical* pesticides are quite worrying.

Side-effects taken from chemical pesticide leaflets

This list of possible side-effects is taken from the Comfortis®
leaflet:

1) Vomiting

2) Depression/lethargy

3) Decreased appetite

4) Poor physical co-ordination

5) Diarrhea

6) Itching

7) Trembling

8) Drooling

9) Seizures

Do not combine the use of generic *ivermectin* at the same time as
Comfortis®.

Do not combine chemical flea-treatments

In cases where dogs have been, 'over-dosed', by a mix of
commercial chemical flea-treatments, some have experienced the
symptoms above *plus* the following:

1) Highly dilated eye-pupils

2) Blindness

3) Disorientation

In the U.K., many Lhasa owners recommend *Stronghold* and others prefer *Advantix*.

There is a noticeable reduction in the flea population during the colder months, so you may choose to reduce the pesticide treatments in cold seasons.

How to choose the best chemical flea-killer?

It is advisable to consult an experienced vet, read the contents' lists and find out about the possible side-effects in order to determine which chemical flea-killer offers the best option.

This is another area in which your puppy's breeder can often provide invaluable advice. It is also useful to talk to other Lhasa owners on the Internet. There are a series of online community boards and forums that you can join through which you can connect with other owners.

Alternatively, if you have a local Lhasa owner's club, you should join it and take advantage of the wealth of knowledge shared by experienced owners.

Natural treatments for fleas

Many owners do not like to use poisonous pesticides on their pet's coat and use essential oils to deter fleas.

Here is a list of the natural oils often used to avoid fleas setting up home in the Lhasa Apsos' coat - or if fleas are already there, to drive them away.

a) Cedar-wood oil

b) Eucalyptus oil

c) Peppermint oil

d) Wormwood oil

These oils can be used to deter fleas by putting a few drops on the dog's collar every day or so. You can also make a handy spray with a few drops of the *essential oil* mixed in a large bottle of a carrier-oil, such as a light almond-oil.

This makes a useful spray for your pet's bedding and it is a lovely way to smooth, scent and moisturize your Lhasa's coat, too.

Washing-up liquid kills fleas

Washing-up liquids like, *Fairy*, also have a strong following as a flea-killing treatment. Bathing your dog in a good-quality washing-up liquid, especially one with added lemon oil or any citrus oil, works well.

Make plenty of suds on your dog to kill fleas and let the citrus oils linger to repel *future fleas* looking for a comfortable home.

Home-made citrus-oil flea-killer

You can make your own lemon flea treatment by soaking a chopped up lemon, lime or orange, plus the peel, in boiling water. Cover the container and leave it to soak in the cooled water overnight.

Then dilute it with water and sponge or spray it all over your pet to kill fleas immediately.

Natural flea treatments like citrus do have to be repeated every few days. However, they are safe - with no toxic chemicals or horrifying side-effects on your pet.

Fossilized algae flea-treatment

Diatomaceous earth kills fleas by drying them out. This is a non-toxic, chalky powder containing fossilized algae, which is sprinkled on carpets and lawns. Garden supply stores usually have it in the U.S.

Traditional baking soda flea-killer

If you prefer traditional household remedies, baking soda kills fleas. Mix equal parts of table salt and baking soda together and sprinkle over the carpets. Work the soda in with your feet or a broom until it is no longer visible.

Leave overnight and then vacuum the carpets carefully, going over it more than once. This usually dries up and removes all fleas, without damaging your carpets, your children or your pets.

Nematodes eat fleas

There are also nematode sprays produced for flea killing and general insect-killing. They are completely natural and non-toxic as the live nematodes will eat the fleas and other small insects. You can buy these at garden centers or from stores found on the Internet, specializing in home and garden equipment.

Ear hygiene and grooming

Should you pluck your Lhasa Apso's ear-hairs?

The best way to keep your Lhasas ears clean and free from infection is another dog-care question that has several answers.

After many years of advice to pluck out the thick hair covering the inside of the Lhasas ears, a number of veterinary dermatologists have said that it can do more harm than good.

Plucking hairs out by the roots, leaves a lot of tiny, open wounds where bacteria can easily enter the tender inner ear tissue and start an infection.

1) Careful clipping of any excess hair around the ear-opening is

helpful to maintain ear health and allow you to clean in the outer ear.

2) Bathing with clean water will not cause ear infections. However, water that is contaminated may deposit microbes into the ear and cause an ear-infection.

3) Cotton-wool buds are useful for cleaning the *outer* crevices of the ear. Always avoid poking into the inner ear-canal. You may push dust, wax or bacteria deeper into the body, which is harmful.

4) When choosing a professional groomer, ensure that they never use materials or tools that have been *pre-used* on another dog. This is one of the reasons that dogs develop ear-infections, like the common *pseudomonas* infection.

5) In addition, *pseudomonas* bacteria can be transferred from an infected ear to surfaces on which sterilized tools are placed and then used on your dog. Cross-contamination from an infected ear can be transferred to humans and animals. *Pseudomonas* infection creates a thick, unpleasant-smelling discharge from the infected ear.

How to clean an infected ear

a) Start with the good ear first to avoid cross-contamination.

b) Use a non-stinging ear-cleaner and be very gentle when cleaning an ear with a suspected infection.

c) If the infection is apparent and looks serious, it may be better to leave it alone and contact your vet. Ear problems are often quite difficult to diagnose correctly.

d) Speedy diagnosis and correct medical treatment will stop the problem getting any worse. This saves your pet from suffering what can be a very painful condition.

e) Disinfect everything that may have had contact with the infected ear or been sprayed with droplets from any ear-shaking. This includes: hands, a bath-tub, the taps, any tools, the table, the dog-pen and bedding and the tip of the ear-cleaner bottle.

In addition to ear discharge, other signs of ear problems are redness, itchiness, odor, swollen tissue in outer ear, hair loss on ear-flaps, hard skin-scales or scabs.

Do not be offended if a professional groomer prefers not to clean your dog's ears, because she suspects an infection. This is good practice and shows they care about hygiene in their salon, which is always a good sign.

Plucking your Lhasa's ear-hair

The hair inside each Lhasa Apso's ears does vary in quantity and thickness.

Therefore dogs with fine or scarce ear-hair do not always need to have them plucked to stay clean and hygienic.

On the other hand, some dogs have a thick coat of coarse hair in their ears. Thick, coarse hair can become matted and retain dust, mites and bacteria.

In these dogs, some owners believe that plucking is the best way to keep the ears clean and free from dirt-retaining 'mats'.

However, if you feel you could do this at home, here is a step by-step guide:

Tools for ear-hair plucking

a) Ear-powder such as *Thornit Ear Powder*

b) A pair of sterilized hair tweezers

c) Or a sterilized stainless-steel pet hemostat

A hemostat-clamp looks like scissors with a gripping edge instead of cutting blades.

Steps for ear-hair plucking

1) Apply the ear-powder inside the outer-ear with a very small spoon, avoiding the ear canal opening.

2) Ensure that all of the hair, including the roots, is covered.

3) Wait several minutes for the ear-powder to dry-out the hairs and any mites in there, too.

4) Pluck only a few hairs at a time, to avoid causing pain to your pet.

If you are not confident about the process of plucking your dog's ears, then your vet will provide this service for you.

Ear-powder ingredients

The ingredients of ear-powder are usually zinc oxide, talc, iodoform and boric acid powder.

The drying effect of the ear-powder helps to plug the tiny open wounds in the plucked area and has an antiseptic action, too.

Boric acid powder is also known as Borax and is a natural pesticide and fungicide.

Ears should be quickly checked every couple of days and cleaned often to deter infections, and keep your dog healthy.

Making the coat-partings

Back parting along the spine

Pop your Lhasa up on the grooming table and stand behind her. Then use the last tooth of a metal comb or a blunt knitting-needle to part the hair. Start at the base of the dog's neck and run the comb straight down the spine so the coat drapes down on each side.

To check if the parting is straight, look along the spine once from the back-end and once from the front-end. Lightly flip any 'stray hairs' over to the other side.

Then use coat-conditioner in a spray bottle to lightly mist the coat along the parting, to keep it in place. This helps to keep the parting in place, because your Lhasa will immediately shake herself after being groomed.

Head and neck parting

Part the muzzle-hair evenly with the end-tooth of the comb and move up to between the eyes. Continue over the head and down the neck, where you *should* find the neck-parting meets the back-parting.

Again, flip any wayward hairs over to the correct side of the parting with the comb, knitting-needle or your fingers.

Grooming of feet

The hair growing between the pads of a Lhasa's foot is fast-growing and can be quite long. If you do not trim this hair it will become matted and dirty and can push the pads apart, which is not good for the dog (or your carpets, either).

The good news is that trimming the Lhasa's foot-pads is an easy task.

1) Put your dog on its back or side, and hold a leg gently but firmly to an angle that allows you clear access to the pads. With the hand you are using to hold the leg, use your fingers to spread the pads apart slightly.

2) Trim the hair carefully with clippers or small manicure scissors.

3) As shaggy feet make even the most carefully brushed Lhasa look a little unkempt, just trim the coat around the edge of the feet for a neater look.

4) Using a comb or a small brush, lift the hair up and then comb a first layer of hair down over the foot. Trim this layer keeping it quite close to the shape of the foot.

5) Then brush down a second layer and trim it slightly longer than the first layer. Repeat this layering until the hair on the foot has a neat and rounded shape.

6) Trim all of the feet in this way.

Note: Lhasa's that do not have a thick coat of hair on their feet, can often be trimmed without you needing to cut several thin layers.

On fine hair, you can often just comb all of the hair over each foot and trim it in one go.

Nail Clipping

Lhasas need to have their toe-nails trimmed regularly as long nails are likely to *catch* on fabric in the home or twigs and plant-stems outdoors, causing a painful injury.

Moreover, very long nails can begin to pierce the foot-pads, causing pain and infection.

Although your playful Lhasa may be accustomed to being handled, they are never very keen to have their paws touched.

This makes the necessary task of nail-clipping a grooming project to approach with these pre-planned strategies.

'Softly, softly' approach

You have to be fairly crafty to begin with and distract your pet with toys, food or frequent pats or stroking of the head during the nail-trimming session.

It is highly recommended that you spend time every day stroking and massaging your dog's feet, right from the beginning.

Then when your pet is used to this, you can start by trimming a couple of nails one day and a couple more the next day.

Trimming needs to begin at an early age and you can build-up to cutting all the nails in one session over a period of time.

The idea is to get her used to nail-trimming gradually, while she is a puppy, so she will not make a fuss about it as an adult.

Best positions for nail-trimming

You may find it helpful to have one person holding your pet, while you do the trimming. Choose someone whom the dog already knows and respects to be the 'holder'.

The holder needs to be calm and confident, to avoid making your pet anxious. Lhasa Apsos are less likely to struggle free if they respect the person holding them.

The 'hold' should not be forced on an unwilling dog or be any type of heavy restriction.

If you make her feel fear, she will *learn* that having her nails trimmed is a negative experience and be even more averse to having her nails trimmed.

The aim is to reduce stress and show your dog that nothing 'bad' is going to happen. Therefore, stroke and gently pat her head frequently to help her feel calm.

Back or side position

You will need to experiment with different positions to find what works best for all concerned.

Some Lhasas respond well to lying on their side during nail-trimming.

Others prefer to be held in the air vertically, with the foot-pads facing the person wielding the nail-clippers.

A few Lhasas do better and struggle less if they are standing on the ground during their manicure.

If all else fails

Some Lhasa Apsos never become accustomed to nail-trimming at home, or by a grooming professional.

In these cases, a vet will be the best person to keep your pet's nails properly maintained. A few dogs need to be tranquillized before their nails can be cut.

This underlines the importance of patience and gentleness when habituating your puppy to having her paws touched – it is definitely the most *cost-efficient* approach.

Lhasa Apso Hairstyles

Pinning the eye-fall off the face

There are lots of simple and attractive ways to keep the eye-fall hair out of your Lhasa's eyes. For instance, on dogs that do not have a thick eye-fall, you can use hair-slides. Just brush the eye-fall hair back from the face and keep it in place with one hair-slide in the center on top.

Or you can part the hair in the middle and brush each section back fastening with matching hair-slides.

Covered pony-tail elastics are handy for making a sweet little topknot on the top of your Lhasa's head. Many owners prefer the covered 'pony-tail' elastics to small latex elastic bands, as they are more comfortable to wear and don't hurt when you remove them.

Small elastic bands can be made too tight, giving your Lhasa Apso a headache, pulling hairs out from the roots and generally damaging the hair.

Pig-tails are another favorite Lhasa Apso grooming style. This is done by parting the hair in the center and making a little pig-tail on each side of the head.

Braiding/plaiting the eye-fall

1) Braiding/plaiting your Lhasa Apso's eye-fall is another option for those who enjoy grooming Lhasa Apsos to look and feel their best.

2) Before you begin, you need to have a spray bottle of water, coat oil or diluted coat conditioner.

3) If the braid sticks out, it is probably too tight. You may have put too much hair into the plait or you may have started plaiting with the hair pulled out at right-angles to the head. If this happens, gently undo the braiding and start again.

4) Part your pet's hair in the center of the head.

5) Then begin on one side with a light spray of water, coat oil or diluted coat conditioner.

6) Brush it through to avoid tangles and then divide the hair into three equal sections.

7) Start plaiting the three sections by taking the section next to the eye and moving it over the middle section. The braid should

stay close to the head as you continue to the ends of the hair. Fasten the ends with a small elastic band.

8) Plaits usually last a few days, before they need to be brushed out and re-done. Try not to leave plaits in for more than 4 - 5 days without undoing and brushing through the hair, for your Lhasa's comfort and to prevent matting.

9) Generally you can section each side from a point between each eye's center and outside corner. Take the section about 2 inches/50 cm back. The thickness of each section of the plait depends on the thickness of your dog's eye-fall, so just experiment until the braid suits your dog's head size.

Do Lhasa Apsos shed their hair according to the season?

No. However, there is a one-time, natural change to their coat as they grow from puppies to adolescents. Therefore, if you notice that your Lhasa puppy seems to be *ballooning-out* at the sides, 'Don't Panic.'

This is exactly how they look when the stronger adult coat is growing and your puppy is ready to shed its softer hair. The best way to deal with this process is by frequent grooming, so read on for more information on how to be completely prepared.

Coping with Coat Change in Lhasa Apso Puppies

The average age for coat change is between 9 – 14 months. However, each dog is an individual and the change can begin as early as 6 months or not until 16 months.

A responsible breeder will probably have explained how to cope with the change from puppy coat to adult coat. In case you have forgotten what they said, here is the best way to groom your *pudgy-looking* puppy during this time – without having to take a hopelessly matted Lhasa to the grooming salon and begging them to, 'clip it all off.'

Daily 'coat-change' grooming

During the coat change period, the puppy hair ceases to be renewed by the body and becomes loose, ready for shedding. This means it needs frequent daily brushing-out to remove the surplus hair, or you will be faced with a terribly tangled mat.

How long does 'coat-change' take?

The Lhasa Apso puppy's coat-change takes place over about four weeks and daily grooming is vital at this time. Do not be surprised at the size of the large piles of hair you will be removing each day. Providing it is all soft, puppy hair, this is all normal, even if it may seem a little alarming at times.

Remember that the tough-textured adult coat is a lot easier to groom, so use this fact to help keep motivated and encouraged during the labor intensive and frequent grooming periods, which can be strenuous at times.

Keep on top of the job.

If you do not have the time to brush your Lhasa completely every day, at least do some grooming on the insides of the legs, the neck and behind the ears.

Avoid leaving a full brushing more than two days, though, as the hairs hiding in the undercoat will be getting very tangled and matted, even if the top coat looks fine.

Early training makes grooming easier

This is another reason why it is essential to train your Lhasa to accept being handled and groomed from the start. Otherwise you will both struggle to complete this important stage in your beautiful Lhasa's development.

Chapter Eight: Socialization & House-Training

Socialization is an important aspect of your puppy's life and it actually starts from the moment he is born. Before he comes home with you, your breeder has probably already been socializing your puppy.

Puppies raised in a home learn about vacuums, televisions, music, meet people and get lots of love and petting from the moment they are born.

Most breeders will take puppies outside to let them experience the grass and other surfaces. Puppies usually go to the vet and meet some friendly strangers there.

In addition, your Lhasa Apso puppy's mother and littermates will also teach him puppy manners, so he has some idea of how to behave with other dogs.

Your key role in socializing

Between 3 - 8 weeks of age, your puppy will have been socialized at the breeder's home.

However, after you take your puppy home, it is up to you to continue to socialize your Lhasa. This is especially important with the Lhasa breed, which is reserved and suspicious of people because of their watch-dog heritage.

However, between 8 -16 weeks, you need to make time to work on socialization. The logic behind this is that puppies are less fearful and more open to new experiences at this time.

The cautious stage

The puppy will start becoming more cautious about new things between the approximate age of 7 – 9 weeks (some puppies earlier and some later than this) and this makes socialization more difficult.

The main problem with this restricted 8 – 16 weeks age-period is the fact that your Lhasa Apso cannot go to many places, until it has had the second set of vaccinations.

Therefore, *your* role in the socialization process is vital to your puppy's future health and happiness.

Puppy-training classes

Most professional dog-trainers recommend puppy classes after 16 weeks of age and do not start socialization until after those classes begin.

However, although puppy classes are strongly recommended for this breed, you should be socializing your puppy well before 16 weeks.

How to begin socializing your puppy

During the first few weeks at home, from 8 to 16 weeks, take the time to socialize your puppy to a range of different stimuli in the home.

For example, continue to expose your puppy to the same things he probably experienced at the breeder's home.

This includes machines such as a vacuum cleaner, television, music, noise from the washing machine and visitors to your home.

Make sure that you touch your puppy and handle him often, so he can become accustomed to your touch.

After your puppy is 12 weeks old, or has had his second set of vaccinations, take him to places where puppies and small dogs are welcome and continue his socialization with other dogs.

Puppies will continue to go through different stages as they grow and develop, including more fear stages.

The critical fear periods in puppies

a) Seven to nine weeks

b) Four to six months

c) Approximately eight to nine months

d) Approximately twelve months

e) Approximately fourteen to eighteen months

During these stages your puppy can be fearful of people, places and objects that he already knows. He might bark at very ordinary things.

He might shake or hide from something that would not normally bother him. This is all normal behavior for your puppy during these stages and you can help like this:

1) Stick to familiar routines during these times

2) Reward positive behavior and try not to encourage fearful behavior

What Should I Socialize To?

You may be wondering what you should use for socializing your puppy. While everyone has different living circumstances that will change your socialization stimuli, there are a number of stimuli that you should use for your puppy no matter where you live. Below is a checklist to get you started with socializing your Lhasa Apso:

Stimuli	X	Stimuli	X
Men: Bearded and clean-shaven		Balls of various size	
Women		Mirrors	
Children: Boys and Girls		Baby strollers	
Toddlers: Boys and Girls		Grocery carts	
Babies: Boys and Girls		Mirrors	
People with glasses		Brooms	
People with crutches		Dusters	
People with canes		Vacuum cleaners	
People in wheelchairs		Wind	
Slouched people		Flags	
People with walkers		Tents	
Shuffling people		Flashlights	

Large crowds		Children's Toys	
Small crowds		Television	
People on roller blades		Plastic bags	
People of various shapes and sizes: tall, thin, heavy, short, etc.		Umbrellas	
People with sunglasses		Balloons	
People who are exercising		Skateboards	
People on bikes		Children playing	
Costumes		Hammering	
Bald people		Construction equipment	
Big dogs		Lawn mowers	
Little dogs		Scooters	
Farm animals		Buses	
Puppies		Trains	
Small Rodent/non canine		Sirens	
Birds		Ceiling fans	
Lizards		Garage doors	
Escalators		Dremel tools	
Cars: Both while walking and riding in them		Fireworks	
Sliding doors		Cheering	
Planes (optional)		Yelling	
Elevators		Radios	
Escalators		Storms	
Alarms		Loud noises	
Singing		Visiting the vet	

Grooming		Getting nails cut	
Being crated		Being picked up	
Having all body parts touched		Leash	
Collar		Harnesses	

Lhasa Apsos and visitors to your home

Children

As already mentioned, Lhasas are not suitable for homes where there are young children. They are fine with responsible older children, but in a home where your children's friends are frequent visitors, some training is necessary – for all concerned. You will have to introduce frequent visitors of any age to your Lhasa individually, so it is clear who is 'friend' and who is 'foe'.

Infrequent visitors

Repair men/women, party guests and other less frequent visitors will also have to be formally introduced to your Lhasa. Ask them to give your dog a pat or two and a food treat supplied by you and stand close to your visitor to show your dog they are welcome in your home.

Social training with other dogs

Take your puppy to basic obedience classes, where your standoffish puppy will meet other dogs and learn social etiquette. The more social opportunities you provide for your Lhasa, the better he will be with other dogs in general.

Lhasas are naturally territorial in the home, but on neutral ground they are more open to new people and pets. If you have a local dog-walking area, that's the best way to let your Lhasa mix with other dogs. However, avoid areas where there are large dogs and for safety, always stay in the area reserved for small dogs

House-training basics

If you are attentive to your puppy's toileting needs and stick to the basics of Lhasa Apso potty-training, he should be fully home-trained by the age of 5 - 6 months.

Some Lhasas need extra reinforcement during adolescence or in adulthood, so be prepared to keep them to a tight schedule and watch them carefully when indoors at this time.

House-training your Lhasa Apso puppy will be easier if you have purchased from a responsible breeder. This will mean your puppy is used to a clean living space. If you stick closely to this house-training schedule for Lhasas, you should not have much difficulty.

Key toileting times

When house-training your Lhasa, the key element is being consistent and sticking to a regular timetable – while staying friendly and having a good sense of humor. Allow your puppy access to an outdoor location where she can relieve herself soon after:

a) eating,

b) waking from a nap

c) a play session

With a little planning, you will soon be able to arrange your own necessary outdoor trips to fit in with your Lhasa's house-training time-table.

At the age of 12 weeks, Lhasa Apso pups can be expected to wait overnight. However, they do not have the same amount of bladder control as an adult, so it is your responsibility to supervise your puppy during the day, to prevent 'accidents'.

Supervision and creating a safe, clean space

One of the best house-training tools is a dog-pen, which creates a safe, small space that a puppy from a good breeder should want to be clean.

It is not in any way cruel to use a pen to protect your puppy from getting into a dangerous situation when you are not supervising its behavior directly.

Although you should be cautious about training your Lhasa Apso puppy solely with food treats, a puppy will learn to walk into a dog-pen quite happily if you give it a treat as soon as it enters - for the first few times.

Stop boredom in crated dogs

To keep your puppy occupied while in the pen, give it a toy or some puppy food pushed into a hollow steamed bone, so it has to work at getting the food out.

If your puppy is barking, do not rush to let it out of the crate immediately, as this will only teach it that barking is a good way to control you.

Instead, wait for the puppy to stop barking - and then add on a few seconds to be sure your Lhasa knows who is boss - before opening the pen and taking him swiftly outside to the toilet area.

House-training - getting started

After the upset of moving to a new home, the puppy will probably want to use the toilet right away.

1) Before you buy the puppy, it's recommended for you to choose a suitable spot for toileting it.

2) As soon as you arrive home, take your puppy to this spot. It will sniff around a little and you need to praise it for this. Let the puppy relieve itself in the chosen spot, keep praising it and give a 'positive reinforcement' reward of its favorite food treat.

3) Afterwards, follow a timetable of allowing your puppy about 20 minutes of 'supervised freedom' indoors, before taking it back to the toilet spot. If no use is made of the toilet area, pop your puppy back into the pen for a nap and when it wakes up take it to the toilet area again.

4) If you see your puppy preparing to urinate or evacuate indoors, just scoop it up and take it straight to the outdoor toilet spot.

5) Keep the toilet area clean.

6) Continue to praise your dog for sniffing and using the designated 'toilet area', until this behavior becomes automatic for your dog.

Note: Never play with your puppy *before* it uses the toilet, wait until it has done its duty and then have fun together.

How to deal with 'accidents'

If you discover your puppy has had an 'accident' in the home when you were not looking, punishing him afterwards will not achieve anything. Your pet has no way of linking the two events and will be confused.

Clean up the mess *without* letting your puppy see you and always take him outside immediately if he returns to the 'accident' site and starts to sniff it.

As Lhasas begin to understand the toileting time-table, you can allow them progressively longer periods of indoor free-time. However, it is your responsibility to watch your pet all the time, for several months, as it gradually gains control of its elimination habits.

More house-training tips – tether training

If an adolescent or adult Lhasa Apso starts having accidents in the home, you can attach the lead and fasten it to a belt around your waist.

This is generally known as, 'tether-training' and it lets you supervise your dog every minute, until the official toilet break.

It is a good way to stop any sneaking off behind the sofa and helps build the bond between you and your pet.

Nappies for older pups or ageing dogs

Another way to prevent accidents indoors is to place a nappy on your older puppy or adult.

Lhasas do not like the cold dampness of a soiled nappy and this encourages them to wait for a toilet break, when you remove the nappy and take them outside. If you try this, remember to cut a hole for the tail.

When to consult your vet about poor response to house-training

If you have been carefully following this 'potty-training' guide for two or three weeks, but your puppy's toilet habits have not improved, you should take your Lhasa to see a vet.

It is always a good idea to check there is no physical problem interfering with your pet's house-training.

Dealing with adolescent territory-marking behavior

Adolescent males that have not been neutered retain the instinct to mark their territory. They do this by leaving little spots of urine around the home.

One of the best ways to avoid this is to have your male neutered well before adolescence begins. The best age to have your male neutered is between 4 – 6 months.

Older males that 'mark' territory with urine

If you have an older male with marking problems, the 'belly-band' used with tether-training helps to re-train your pet.

A belly-band is a strip of cloth that can be wrapped around the trunk and fastened with Velcro. The cloth is lined with a women's panty-liner and although the dog will still try to leave urine spots, the liner will absorb it.

Use correction at the same time to make a permanent change in this behavior. This should be a short, sharp pull on the lead accompanied by a specific voice cue. For instance, 'Don't mark.'

Rescue dogs marking

Sometimes adult rescue dogs forget their house-training or try to mark their new home. Body-bands are helpful while they are settling in to a strange, new environment, too.

Females marking

In addition, females occasionally start 'marking' their territory. Tether-training and voice cue will also teach her not to do this. For further details on tether-training, refer to the house-training your puppy section, in this chapter.

Older Lhasas and incontinence

Spayed females and neutered males sometimes go on to develop incontinence. Do not get upset if this happens, as it can easily be controlled by medication from the vet.

Lhasas recovering from surgery to treat bladder conditions or kidney stones have their own set of problems.

It is normal for them to lack full control until the bladder or kidneys heal and this should be treated with patience and understanding.

As always, if you do not see this situation improving after a couple of weeks, consult your vet to see if anything is amiss.

Stages of Life

On average, smaller dogs mature slower and live longer than larger breeds. However, every Lhasa Apso develops and ages at its own rate and a lot depends on the diet you feed your dog.

How long each life-stage lasts

a) Puppyhood ends between 6 and 18 months of age

b) Adolescence starts between 6 and 18 months of age

c) Adulthood starts between 12 – 18 months

d) The senior years begin between 6 and 10 years of age

Keep in mind

During adolescence, Lhasas may indulge in 'marking' their 'territory' by trying to urinate in the home.

Therefore, you will need to watch your 'watch-dog' more closely for a few months, to make sure he does not get away with this breach of the house-training rules. Many people deal with this habit by using the previously mentioned dog body-band.

The dog still tries to deposit urine in your home, but it is all absorbed by the panty-pad.

Chapter Nine: Training your Lhasa Apso

We will cover training your Lhasa Apso in this chapter. However, it does not replace the advice and training of a Certified Professional Dog Trainer. If your means allow for it, we strongly suggest you enroll your Lhasa Apso puppy in puppy kindergarten or puppy pre-school classes. We encourage you to follow up with a good basic obedience class when your puppy is a little older. This will also offer ample socialization to your puppy.

Also, should you wish to use one, please do research when hiring a trainer. Not all dog trainers are created equal. Ask about continuing education and any certifications they may have, and what they must do to keep them current. Dog training is a totally unregulated field and anyone at all can call themselves a dog trainer and not be accountable to anyone. There had even been a case of a pet dying from abuse resulting from poor "training" in New Jersey, U.S.

So it is best to seek out a trainer who is certified by an independent certifying body that is not monetarily motivated by any manufacturers of training equipment or food. Two fine examples are CCPDT (the Certification Council for Professional Dog Trainers) or IAABC (International Association of Animal Behavior Consultants).

Training Basics

It is important to actively work to engage your Lhasa Apso in a way that is both fulfilling and understandable to him or he will quickly lose interest and find something else to do. This is best achieved with the use of a clicker or the word 'Yes!' as a marker of good performance.

Always use a marker to inform the dog that he has performed correctly. You must pair the marker word or the click with the treats by repeatedly clicking or saying the marker word as you deposit treats in the dog's mouth. Through this technique, the dog will learn that the click or the marker word means a treat.

This is necessary in order to communicate to the dog that he has done something correct at the occurrence of the desired behavior. Remember, dogs only have a memory of their own behavior for approximately half a second after the behavior has occurred.

Therefore, it is essential that we have a way to communicate good performance on the instant that it happens in order for the dog to understand that it has done something well. This is why it is best to use a clicker or a marker word to achieve this rather than trying to deliver a treat within half a second of the correct behavior. One would have to be a veritable ninja with treats to make this work without the marker!

You can then apply the clicker or the marker word to teaching your Lhasa Apso any type of behavior, such as a collar grab. To do this, every time you reach down and touch the collar, click or say the marker word and give your dog a treat.

The reason for the latter is to let your dog know that touching the collar is not bad. Often, when we give a cue, such as 'come', 'sit' or 'heel', it is because we want to gain control of them. If we don't train a dog to become familiar with having their leash touched, the dog may get into the habit of running from you when you go to grab his collar.

Molly Sumner, A Certified Professional Dog Trainer (Certified Canine Behavior Consultant and Certified Behavioral Adjustment Training Instructor), from New Jersey, U.S. has some useful insights about training. When asked what the key to training this breed is, she had this to say:

"I think there are a few elements that are more important than any others. First, you need a clicker. It's a very distinctive sound that when paired effectively with the right food reward, serves as the best communication tool available. You also need to understand that reinforcement is a far larger category than just food. You need the patience of a saint and you need to be 100% committed to getting what you want. Maybe not today, maybe not tomorrow, maybe not next week, but eventually. However long that might be. You need the animal to trust you completely, not just to give rewards, but to step in and remove things that are making it uncomfortable or remove the animal if it becomes too agitated. Feeling safe and secure is extremely important for a primitive breed." - Molly Sumner.

Taking that excerpt piece by piece, we will discuss the clicker or the "Yes!" marker first.

1) Have a great deal of treats in your treat pouch or in a bowl out of the dog's reach.

2) Click the clicker and/or say the "Yes!" marker at the same time as you deposit a treat in the dog's mouth.

3) Repeat this continuously, as fast as you can for about 5 to 10 minutes a day for the first week and then once a week thereafter to maintain the association.

If you do this consistently, you will have trained a very effective reward marker and your dog will think the clicker or the word "Yes!" is the best thing ever and a motivating sound in its own right.

What she means by patience is that training doesn't happen in a day or even a week or a month. If the dog just isn't grasping "Down", keep trying. If you still can't get it, do something the dog does know, reward for that, and come back to "Down" later. By staying "100% committed to getting what you want." She means that these dogs learn more from us than we think. If, in the end, not the beginning, you settle for less than what you want; the dog will learn that it doesn't actually have to perform correctly at all.

Remember, if you miss that half-second window immediately after the desired behavior has been performed, the dog will be confused as to why it earned the treat. There also must be a relationship of trust between you. The dog needs to be secure in the knowledge that you will not place him in an uncomfortable situation and just expect him to "deal with it." You must make every effort to manage his state of mind if you want the best results.

Before you start training your puppy or dog, ensure that you accept that this process may take some time. You should adjust your expectations and be happy with small degrees of progress. They are smart dogs and they can learn quickly. Whether they choose to obey you is another matter. This is where your relationship and trust with your Lhasa Apso become important. If your dog can trust you completely to pay him for his work, and make it fun, then you will have little trouble motivating him.

With that said, do not imagine for one moment that you can bully this breed into compliance. Lhasa Apsos expect to be companions and partners. The best policy is calm insistence on what you want and never giving up on it. Even if it means revisiting it in order to achieve the desired result.

Rules

The Lhasa Apso does require rules and it is of dire importance that you be consistent with them. Before you bring your puppy home, think of the rules that you want to have in your house. If you are fine with dogs on the furniture, allow it. If not, don't allow it from the very moment your puppy comes home. It may not seem like a big deal but it will confuse your Lhasa Apso when you finally tell him to stay off. When you are training your Lhasa Apso, be sure to follow these rules:

Rule Number One: Manners

Always insist on manners. Never under any circumstances allow a puppy to practice behaviors that you would find undesirable in an adult dog. This means that jumping up should never be practiced. If the puppy does jump up, even once, turn your back on him and make like a tree.

Removing your attention from a puppy is a more effective discourager than anything else. If the puppy still continues to jump, confine them to another area and try again in a few minutes. The rule is that the puppy may not get away with poor manners. This is a good time to ask for a sit and reward instead of jumping. Remember, give the puppy something it can get right.

Rule Number Two: Make him Work

Regardless of whether you are giving him food, a treat or praise, you want your dog to work for it. Always give your Lhasa Apso a cue, such as "sit" and "wait" at dinner-time, before you give him some form of reward. This will teach him that he needs to work for things and will also help with manners so he is not jumping or grabbing at things.

Rule Number Three: Be the Initiator

Playing, cuddling, and any type of attention should be done with you initiating it. Pick up toys, although you can leave out a few to combat chewing, and bring them out for play sessions.

Do not give in if he brings the toys to you and is pushy in forcing you to play. In addition, don't pay attention to your Lhasa Apso if he is jumping or biting at you to get attention. Instead, ignore him until he is sitting politely and then give him the attention.

Rule Number Four: Give your Lhasa Apso his own Space

While it can be tempting to keep your dog with you at all times, make sure that you give him his own space as well. Crate training is recommended since it keeps puppies from chewing when you aren't home. You can also give your dog his own bed area.

This area will give him a chance to take a break when the house is too busy or he is tired. In addition, it will be a safe place for him and that will help in establishing roles in your home. Not only will he feel secure in such a place, but also with his role in the house.

Rule Number Five: Always have Access to his Food

Finally, always make sure that you have access to your dog's food dish. When he is a puppy, take the time to have your hands in his dish and also make sure that you feed him a few handfuls.

If your Lhasa Apso becomes too pushy when you are in the dish, lift it up and only feed him by hand when he relaxes.

You also want to teach him that the food will be given back to him so that he has no need to feel that it is lost to him. Always give treats when interacting with the food dish! Have everyone in the house do the food dish exercise. It helps with preventing food guarding or aggression.

Lhasa Apsos often tend to have issues about food. They can guard their food, dump their food, try to gulp it all down at one go, and show other extraordinary behaviors. You may have to work on your puppy's food issues from a young age to help him relax about them.

In the end, when you are training your Lhasa Apso, it comes down to being consistent, firm and making it fun. If you do that, along with providing firm, calm insistence on the behavior you want, you will make progress with training your Lhasa Apso.

Training your Lhasa Apso

This section is about the essential cues that your Lhasa Apso should know and how to teach them.

It is also necessary to recognize that dogs do not understand the concept of "No." They do what they do for their own reasons. Trying to tell them that they are wrong for doing it simply doesn't compute. The reason for this is that the word 'no', does not simply mean 'no', it is a negative word thrown at anything one might say 'no' to.

Dogs need the English words we teach them to have only one definite meaning. 'No' has as many meanings as you can think to apply it to. Therefore, it is impossible for a dog to grasp a concept that is so global and all-encompassing in scope. This is the basis of why we no longer correct dogs for improper performance.

We recommend using a small treat that is soft and does not require a lot of chewing for training. Hard treats that need to be chewed break the training session regularly. The dog has to focus more on chewing than on training.

Chicken nuggets or Frankfurters make excellent small treats. Slice them into pieces that are no larger than half the size of your small finger nail. These treats are rich in flavor, and are easy to chew.

It's important that the treats are small because you don't want your dog to fill up too quickly. You need him to stay hungry long enough to pay attention for the entire time you are training. On the same note, do not feed your dog a big meal just before you start to train him or he won't be interested in your treats. In fact, he will probably feel like taking a nap.

This part is critically important: You must avoid baiting or bribing your Lhasa Apso into anything except when first learning a behavior. As soon as he grasps what is being asked of him, remove all treats from your hands. You can achieve this by using a treat pouch when you are out or keeping treats high up on shelving when you are home. This is necessary because the dog must be willing to work for a reward and this takes time to teach.

If you continue to bribe a dog for performing, his performance will become dependent on the presence of the bribe. This will not occur if your dog understands the concept of rewards and can trust you to reward him once he has done something right. Performance need not be dependent on the presence of food.

When you are training your Lhasa Apso, keep him on the leash the entire time unless you are practicing off-leash lessons. This will prevent him from wandering away when he is bored. (Hopefully your dog won't get bored with your lessons.)

In addition, never give the cue more than once. If you do this, your Lhasa Apso will decide that he doesn't have to listen.

Essential Cues

"Sit!"

"Sit" is one of the first cues your Lhasa Apso will need to learn. To train "sit," do the following:

1) Have your dog stand in front of you so he is facing you.

2) Place a treat in your right hand and place it near his nose. Do not let him pounce at the treat.

3) Give the cue, never repeat the cue, just say it once, "Sit."

4) Take the treat up and over his head slowly. His muzzle should follow and his bottom should drop. Use the click or the marker word to tell him he is right the instant his bottom touches the

ground

5) BE PATIENT, it may take a while to achieve the behavior you want. NEVER force your Lhasa Apso to do anything as this will engage his oppositional reflex and this will shut down any learning that might have occurred.

6) Just be patient and persistent. If it just isn't working, come back to it after a relaxing break.

7) Never punish or correct your Lhasa Apso for an incorrect behavior. This will sour him on the learning experience and can lead to very serious behavioral issues later in life.

If you are having too much difficulty teaching your Lhasa Apso the necessary cues, please contact a Certified Professional Dog Trainer for help.

"Stay!"

"Stay" is another cue that is taught when your puppy is young. It is an important cue that can be used in conjunction with a number of different cues. To train "stay", do the following:

 Ask for a "sit" and reward when you receive one. Say the cue word, "stay" and place your hand in front of his nose, palm facing the dog. Count one second and click or say the marker word and give a treat. Gradually increase the duration of the "stay" by waiting three or four seconds between giving the cue and marking then treating. Once he has completed the "stay" successfully several times, start adding distance in by taking a small step backward after you give the "stay" cue.

1) If he doesn't move, take a step back and praise him, touch his collar and treat him.

2) Repeat the process, slowly going further away from him and making him wait for longer as the training progresses.

If he breaks the "stay", do not correct or punish, simply reset the "stay" at an easier level and then work the treats back in. Your calm persistence and clear communication will pay off.

"Down"

Teaching "down" refers to teaching your Lhasa Apso to lie down. This should be taught after your dog has learned the "sit" cue since you will often put them into a "down" from a "sit," especially when they are first learning the cue. To train "down," do the following:

1) Ask the dog for a "sit" so he is facing you. Mark and reward that "sit".

2) Place a treat in your right hand and place it near his nose. Do not let him reach for the treat. Slowly move the treat from his nose to his front toes. He should fold right into a down after a few tries. If you are not having any success, just be patient and stick with it. Your persistence will pay off.

3) When he finally does put his front elbows on the floor, mark the behavior with a click or the marker word and deliver a treat. Repeat several times.

4) When the dog has grasped this maneuver, name the behavior with the "Down" cue. To do this, just say the word "down" as you are clicking or marking on the instant the front elbows touch the ground and the dog is lying down.

5) Gradually begin to say the "down" cue sooner, just before the elbows touch the ground. Continue to click or mark and treat as

soon as his elbows touch the ground. As the dog is more successful, begin to say the "down" cue sooner and sooner.

In no time, you will have a good grasp of the "down" cue.

6) Remember, this can take weeks of trying for some Lhasa Apsos to learn. Never use force to mould a Lhasa Apso into position.

7) When he is lying down, give the dog praise, touch his collar and treat him.

"Come"

This is one of the most important cues that you can teach your Lhasa Apso, and is also one of the hardest. This is the cue where you will need to have some trust in your dog. However, when you are first training your Lhasa Apso, you will need to keep him on the leash.

When you are teaching "come," it is important to never use the cue for punishment. What this means is that you should never tell your Lhasa Apso to "come" when he has done something wrong, and then punish him when he does. He will learn that "come" is a bad thing and won't "come" at any other time.

Instead, make it the most wonderful thing that your dog can do. Heap praise on him and give him lots of treats. To encourage your Lhasa Apso to "come", clap your hands, be exciting and interesting and he will come running.

You can train "come" in two different ways, one is when you place him in a "sit" and "stay," and then call him to "come." This is a focused "come" and while it is useful, it shouldn't be the only way you teach "come." Remember that 90% of the time, your dog will need to come when there is something more interesting to look at.

The other way to train "come" is when he is distracted. This can be taught on a leash as well. To do any type of leash training to "come," you should do the following:

1) Place your dog on the leash. Either have him do a "sit"-"stay" or let him forage out ahead of you. I recommend using a 50 foot lead for this so you can introduce "come" at different distances.

2) If he is in a "sit"-"stay," walk away from the dog and then give the cue for "come." If he is forging ahead, wait until your Lhasa Apso is distracted.

3) Give the cue, "come," and then encourage the dog to come to you by clapping your thighs, being excited and so on. Wave a treat out for him. Do not repeat the cue.

4) Simply walk in the opposite direction. This may pull the leash tight, but remember, once the dog decides to join you, shower him with praise and treats.

5) When the dog reaches you, either on his own or by being reeled in, use the treat to guide him into a "sit" without giving the cue.

6) Praise the dog, touch his collar and treat.

7) Continue training "come" over several weeks. After your puppy becomes adept at "come" at a few feet, increase the distance slightly. The goal is to work up until he can be 100 or more feet from you and still "come" when called, whether on the leash or off.

"Heel"

Many owners have problems with dogs that drag them down the street, pulling their arms out of their sockets, and tangling leashes around legs. It can be dangerous to take a walk with some dogs because of this.

Heeling and walking on a loose leash are two different things. Heeling is more formal and it requires the dog to walk politely at your left side, at knee-level, and sit when you stop walking. It is a cue that is often seen in obedience classes and obedience tests.

Walking on a loose leash is a more informal cue in which the dog walks politely on the leash without pulling, and is not required to stay exactly by the owner's leg, or to sit when the owner stops walking, but he must not pull on the leash or be rambunctious. A well-trained dog should be able to heel when asked and always walk on a loose leash at other times.

We'll go over training for both of these cues. Heeling first:

To teach your Lhasa Apso to heel you should do the following:

1) Put him on the leash.

2) Set off walking with him on your left side and give the "heel" cue.

3) You should have a large cooking spoon in your left hand. The spoon should contain peanut butter, cream cheese, or some other soft treat that will stay on the spoon. Keep the spoon raised.

4) Every two or three steps lower the spoon and allow your Lhasa Apso to lick the soft treat. Then raise the spoon. Do not break your stride. Continue walking

5) Stop walking. When you are first teaching this cue, you will need to give your dog the "sit" cue when you stop. Eventually he should sit on his own each time you stop.

6) When you stop and your dog sits, let him lick the spoon again. Praise him.

7) Give the "heel" cue and start walking again. Repeat.

This is a very popular method of teaching dogs to heel, and it works. Your dog will be glued to your side while you have that spoon – long enough to learn the cue and what it means. You can gradually stop using the spoon and the soft treat. This method is a lot more fun for your dog than the endless repetitions of the traditional way of teaching a dog to heel, or using a corrective collar.

Walking on a loose leash

Walking on a loose leash is not a cue as much as it is an expectation. We all expect our dogs to have good manners. This includes when we are out in public with them, walking down the street or visiting someone.

Leash skills begin in puppyhood. This is where your puppy will learn what a leash is and how to behave while on it and off it. There are several rules to follow when teaching a puppy basic leash manners.

First, understand that the leash works both ways. Yet it should never be used as a communication device by jerking or hauling the puppy around with it. If you jerk or haul with the leash, the puppy will learn that the leash means negative actions are on the way.

Second, always treat the leash like a piece of thread; as if it will snap if it is pulled too hard either by the puppy or by you. This will establish an understanding between you and your puppy that goes something like this. "I won't pull the leash too hard if you don't pull the leash too hard." Once this is understood, everything else becomes much easier.

Finally, refrain from using your arm muscles to manipulate the leash. Instead, it is much better to plant your hand in one position (such as your belt line) and use your body to communicate motion to the dog. This is because dogs rarely pay attention to anything above our abdomens. Therefore, it is more effective to use your feet and legs to communicate what you want the puppy to follow, than it is to move your arms.

There are several variations of teaching your dog to walk on a loose leash, and they all use the same principle, that is, keep your dog guessing. Here is the most basic version.

The Three Iron Rules of Loose Leash Walking

There are only three simple rules to follow for loose leash walking.

1) The dog must never be allowed to get away with pulling. If there is pulling, stop the forward motion immediately. The dog may only go forward if he does it nicely.

2) If pulling continues, walk backwards. The dog must learn that pulling gets him the opposite of what he wants. Be careful to never jerk or use your arm muscles to pull the leash. Your rearward motion will do a much better job of convincing the dog to join you.

3) Success depends on utter consistency. If you decide that the

dog can pull because you are heading in that direction anyway, you've just ruined whatever progress you might have made and you must now start again, back at the very beginning.

Advanced Cues

Once your dog has started learning some of the basic cues, you can start adding in some of the more advanced cues. These cues are often useful in everyday life or if you intend to get involved in dog events and activities.

Some of these cues include:

a) Focus or Watch Me

b) Drop it

c) Leave it

These are covered below, and are just a few of the cues you can teach your dog once he knows the basics. You can teach him a wide variety of cues, depending on what you are interested in doing with your dog.

"Focus" (This should ideally be the dog's name).

Not everyone teaches "focus" but it's useful because it is just a quick reminder to the dog that they need to focus on their handler. To teach "focus," all you need is a treat.

1) Have the dog sit or stand in front of you.

2) Place a treat in your hand and place it against his nose. Do not let him take it.

3) Raise the treat slowly to your face, near your eyes.

4) Give the cue, his name or "Focus" or "Watch."

5) When he glances in your eyes, praise and then give the treat.

6) Remove the treat from your hand and continue rewarding for eye contact. You should practice this in different locations, such as the dog park or in your yard. Be sure to remember that he does not have to "come," he just has to pay attention to you. It is acceptable to toss your treat to the dog if he has paid attention to you at distance.

"Drop It!"

"Drop it" can be a life saving cue since it will teach your Lhasa Apso to drop anything that you do not want him to have. "Drop it" is quite easy to teach but you need to set your dog up for the exercise or wait for him to have something that you need to take. To train "drop it," do the following:

1) Have the dog grab something with his mouth. Playing fetch is a great way to encourage this.

2) Once he has something in his mouth, grab it with one hand. In the other, have a treat.

3) Give the cue, "drop It."

4) Place the treat near his nose so he can smell it. He should drop the item.

5) If he does, praise and treat.

6) If he does not drop it, stuff the treat in his mouth behind the object, this will get him to drop it.

7) When he drops the item, act like he did it without having food

inserted into his mouth; praise and treat.

"Leave It!"

"Leave it," like "drop it," is another cue that could save your dog's life. Teaching them to leave things alone on the ground will keep them from eating dangerous items on walks. To teach "leave it," you want to work in stages. Start by leaving things in your hands and then moving up to leaving things on the ground.

1) Place a treat in your hand and close your fist.

2) Hold it in front of your dog and give the cue, "leave it."

3) Allow him to sniff the treat and try to get at it but ignore him when he is doing this.

4) Once he stops, even for a second, praise the dog and give him a treat with your other hand. Do not give the treat from the hand you told him to leave.

5) Repeat.

6) Increase the difficulty as your dog improves with the cue. Place the treat on your open hand, then on the ground under your cupped hand, and then on the ground without your hand covering. Always treat the dog when he visibly leaves the treat when you give the cue.

These are the basics of training your Lhasa Apso. Remember that training lasts the life of your Lhasa Apso and you should spend time everyday working on different lessons, even when he is fully trained.

Chapter Ten: Common Health Problems

General signs of ill-health

Although signs of illness may differ depending on the disease affecting a dog, there are some general signs that you should look out for. When your Lhasa Apso has any of these symptoms, it is important to seek veterinary care.

One thing that must be stressed with any breed is that illnesses are often sudden. It is very easy for a dog to go from healthy to gravely ill quite quickly. Therefore, try to monitor your dog's condition and do daily health checks.

Symptoms that your dog may be sick include:

Bad breath

Bad breath is often a sign of some oral problem but it can also be a sign of other diseases.

If your dog has bad breath, and there is no obvious cause that you can see, make an appointment with your vet.

Stomach upsets

When a Lhasa gets a stomach upset or diarrhea, try feeding several very small meals throughout the day.

This reduces the stress on the digestive system and stops your dog from having an empty stomach. If this does not work, you should consult your vet fairly quickly.

Bile coming up from the stomach can appear as yellow foam around the mouth and signal a serious problem.

Any swelling of the upper gastro-intestinal tract, with yellow foam appearing, can be a sign of a blockage. This could be life-threatening if medical help is not sought immediately.

Drooling

Excessive drooling is a sign that there could be a health problem. If your dog is drooling a lot, make an appointment to see your vet right away.

Loss of Appetite

Loss of appetite is often one of the first indicators that something is wrong with your Lhasa Apso.

With loss of appetite, it is very important to look at the pattern of eating. If your dog is usually a fussy eater, then missing the occasional meal should not give rise to concern.

In addition, if you have a female that has not been spayed, she may stop eating around her heat cycles. Pregnancy can also lead to a dog not eating as much as normal.

The biggest concern is when your dog has not eaten for more than 24 hours, especially if other symptoms are seen.

Excessive Thirst

Apart from hot days when it would be normal to drink more water, if your Lhasa seems to be drinking large amounts of water, it may indicate disease or dehydration.

How much water should a Lhasa drink each day?

In general, a Lhasa should drink about 1 oz. of water for 1 lb. of dog each day and the average adult should weigh roughly 14 – 16 lbs. (6.4 – 8.2 kg).

Changes in Urination

Changes in the color of urine, as well as the frequency of urination, can indicate a health problem.

An increase in urination, or difficulty in urinating, combined with your pet only producing small amounts of urine often indicate illness.

If you spot blood in the urine, contact your vet immediately.

Skin Problems

If your dog's skin appears bright red or you see flaking skin, then it could indicate an underlying health problem.

In addition, if the dog is itching a lot, it could be fleas, mites or an allergy. Consulting the information in this chapter will help you to check the possible reasons for skin problems.

Lethargy and daytime sleeping

Lhasa Apsos like to sleep during the day, but they should not be lethargic. If your dog seems lethargic after having a nap, make sure she is not being over-exercised.

If there is no obvious reason for her being over-tired, contact your vet.

Gum problems and color changes

Although we usually think gum problems are just a sign of gum disease, they can also be linked to other serious diseases in dogs.

Things to look for are:

Swollen Gums: Swollen gums, when accompanied by bad breath, can indicate gum disease or other oral problems.

Bright Red Gums: When a dog's gums are bright red, it could be an indication that the dog is fighting an infection.

Exposure to toxins is another reason for bright red gums. Or your dog could have heatstroke.

Blue Gums: Bluish gums indicate that the Lhasa is lacking oxygen for some reason. Seek immediate veterinarian care.

Purple Gums: Purple gums are often seen when a dog has gone into shock or there is a problem with his blood circulation.

What has happened just before you notice the purple gums in your Lhasa will indicate whether the dog is in shock or not.

Grey Gums: The same as purple gums, when grey gums are seen in a Lhasa, it can indicate either poor blood circulation or shock.

Pale Pink Gums: Pale pink gums can be an indication of anemia.

White Gums: Finally, white gums can be an indication of a loss of blood. This loss can be either externally or internally so contact your vet immediately.

As you can see, gums are one of the primary indicators of illness in dogs. If your dog is a type that normally has black gums, you can check her health by looking at the pink portion of the lower eyelid.

Monitor changes in weight

If you notice unexpected weight loss or weight gain in your Lhasa, there could be an underlying condition.

As soon as you notice unexpected changes in weight, weigh your dog regularly and write the results on a chart. If the trend up or down continues for no obvious reason, contact your vet.

Stiffness of Limbs

Lhasa Apsos are not usually stiff in their limbs. While old age can create some stiffness, there are several diseases that can affect mobility.

If you notice your pet is having difficulty in getting up, climbing stairs or walking, there may be an underlying problem.

Respiratory Problems

Whenever you see excessive sneezing, coughing, labored breathing and panting, take note.

It could be nothing, but respiratory problems are often an early indication that there is a health problem.

Runny Eyes or Nose

If you see any discharge or fluid coming out of your pet's eyes or nose, keep a close watch on her symptoms.

This can be linked to several conditions including respiratory illnesses.

Vomiting and Gagging

Dogs sometimes gag and vomit without being ill.

However, if you see repeated vomiting and your pet is hanging her head low and gagging continuously, seek medical help. Vomiting and gagging can be a sign of allergies or indicate a life threatening disease.

Fluctuations in Temperature

Finally, if you suspect your Lhasa Apso is unwell, it is important to check her temperature.

Temperatures that are too high can indicate a fever, which could be a symptom of a serious disease. Too low a temperature could indicate other problems such as shock.

Check the temperature with a rectal thermometer or an ear thermometer. Make sure that your dog's temperature is between the following ranges:

Rectal Temperature: Rectal temperatures in dogs should be between 100.5°F to 102.5°F (38°C to 39.2°C)

Ear Temperature: Ear temperatures in dogs should be between 100°F to 103°F (37.7°C to 39.4°C)

If the temperature is lower or higher, contact your vet fairly quickly.

It is important to note that if your pet has just *one* of the symptoms above, there may not be a health problem.

Summary

1) If your pet has three or more of the symptoms described above, you should seek medical care promptly.

2) The single exception to the correct temperature rule is pregnant females.

3) For more information on temperature changes in pregnancy, please consult Chapter Thirteen, which discusses breeding.

Known Health Problems of the Breed

The Lhasa Apso breed has two possible deformities, which can cause severe breathing, walking and eye problems.

a) Brachycephalic – breathing problems

b) Chondrodysplasia – deformed legs

BAOS - Brachycephalic Air Obstruction Syndrome

Many Lhasas have some degree of obstruction to their airways, which causes symptoms ranging from noisy breathing to fainting. In severe cases, BAOS affects the heart owing to insufficient oxygen intake.

Signs and symptoms of BAOS

a) Snuffling and snorting to a noticeable degree

b) Increasingly noisy breathing, coughing and gagging

c) Fainting or collapsing

d) Easily tired after short exercise

How to avoid shortness of breath

Overheating is a danger to the Lhasa.

The normal way of cooling down for dogs is panting. However, in the Lhasa, too much panting can cause swelling in the throat and this narrows the airways.

Difficulty in breathing will make your dog more anxious and this will create even more panting and narrowing of the trachea, which often occurs in humans with asthma.

Excitement, exercise and warm temperatures are all triggers to this vicious cycle – especially when they all happen at once.

They can also cause stomach problems, as dogs find it difficult to swallow when they are gasping for breath.

In this situation, a Lhasa may vomit and there is a danger of lung problems like pneumonia. This can result from the dog gasping so much that saliva or bits of food are breathed into the lungs.

Treatment

Oxygen therapy and cortico-steroids give short term relief of swollen airways. Surgery is necessary when the situation becomes severe.

Note: It is important not to let your Lhasa become overweight, as this worsens any breathing difficulties.

Breeding advice

BAOS syndrome is directly related to puppy-farm breeders creating Lhasas that have a very short ('cute-looking') face.

BAOS causes serious physical problems and discomfort for individual dogs. This is another reason to avoid buying from breeders not affiliated to a Lhasa Apso Club or National Kennel Club.

Breed improvement, aimed at avoiding the extremely short fore-face, is encouraged for responsible breeders. Therefore, dogs with obvious breathing difficulties, and those that have needed surgery to correct a severe airway obstruction, should not be used for breeding.

Most affected dogs are neutered at the same time as the corrective surgery.

Legs affected by chondrodysplasia

The extra-long back and short legs of Lhasas can produce pups that are *chondrodysplastic.*

Good breeders are careful to avoid producing puppies with this problem. Therefore, it is normal practice in responsible breeding that:

1) All chondrodysplastic dogs are sterilized

2) All dogs producing a chondrodysplastic puppy are sterilized

3) Litter-mates of all known carriers must either undergo a test to determine if they are carriers or be sterilized

Eye conditions

Eye diseases in Lhasas are not easy to diagnose in puppies and may only appear several years later. For instance:

a) PRA (Progressive Retinal Atrophy) at 3 – 4 years old

b) Cataracts between 3 – 6 years old

Unfortunately, both of these genetic conditions eventually cause blindness. Symptoms include vision problems, walking problems and behavioral problems (including sudden aggression or unprovoked attack behavior)

Progressive Retinal Atrophy (PRA)

It is only during the last few years that medical research has identified Lhasas as one of the many breeds likely to be affected by PRA.

PRA affects the *retina*, which is the thin, light-sensing layer, at the back of the eye.

In affected dogs, the retinal tissue gradually dies off, eventually causing complete blindness.

Affected dogs will have full sight at birth and PRA may not show up until the dog is around 2 ½ - 8 years of age.

PRA eye disease - signs and symptoms

a) The dog does not want to go out at night or is afraid of entering a dark room. This is a symptom that the dog has lost her night vision.

b) When PRA progresses, the dog can go upstairs, but does not want to walk downstairs.

c) A dog will jump up on the sofa or the bed, but must be helped down.

d) You can sometimes see a green or orange reflection from the dog's eyes in dimly-lit conditions.

e) The dog's pupils' are seen to be widely dilated.

f) Some dogs become aggressive when their sight is failing, but most remain sociable.

Atopy – reverse sneezing – allergic sneezing

Reverse sneezing, *atopy*, is more or less the canine form of hay-fever and occurs in about 10% of dogs.

A Lhasa with this condition become sensitive to allergens found in their environment, which can be breathed-in or absorbed through the skin.

Atopy allergy symptoms

Extreme itchiness, *pruritis*, that starts slowly and progresses to become a constant irritation for your Lhasa.

The main allergens causing *atopy* are:

a) home dust-mites

b) dust including discarded human skin cells

c) mould and mildew

d) feathers

e) pollen from trees and certain flowering plants and grasses

Atopic itching starts slowly and gradually worsens

Dermatitis

Atopic dogs are also prone to *seborrhoea*, a chronic form of dermatitis.

In addition, they may develop secondary bacterial skin-infections, as well as yeast *(Malassezia)* infections.

Note: Itching that starts suddenly and worsens rapidly is more likely to be an allergic reaction to flea-bites, scabies or hyper-sensitivity to a medical drug.

Inherited allergies

Lhasas are particularly prone to allergic sneezing and skin reactions. If both parents are allergic, their pups will probably be hypersensitive, too.

Initially, just like hay-fever in humans, it may be linked to the seasons. However, most *atopic* dogs go on to have symptoms throughout the whole year.

The condition may begin between the ages of 1 – 3 years, or as late as 6 – 7 years of age.

Atopy **allergy diagnosis and treatment**

A combination approach is generally the most effective way to manage this condition.

First of all, allergy testing by your vet to identify which substances your dog is most sensitive to is crucial. Then you can exclude or greatly reduce their presence in your home.

Sometimes allergy injections are required to provide long-term relief for your dog through immunotherapy.

Breeding advice

As there is a strong family link to the onset of this allergic condition, it is best not to breed affected dogs, their parents or their siblings.

Eye-cataracts

Cataracts cause the transparent lens of the eye to 'cloud over', making it look white and opaque. It may affect just one small area of the lens or the whole eye.

Complete cataracts, affecting both eyes, usually progress to blindness. However, small cataracts that do not become any larger will not interfere with your dog's vision.

Signs and symptoms of cataracts

Congenital cataracts in a new-born puppy, and those that develop at a young age, may be *re-absorbed*, resulting in improved vision.

However, sometimes this process allows lens material to leak into the eye, which can cause inflammation and in some cases, glaucoma.

You may suspect your dog is having sight problems or notice a milky discoloration in your dog's eyes.

A vet will be able to see if a cataract is there using an ophthalmoscope.

With their acute senses of smell and hearing, dogs can compensate very well for eye-sight problems, especially when in a familiar home.

You can help your visually-impaired dog by keeping to regular exercise routes and maintaining your dog's home consistently.

Dogs with cataracts benefit from patience and understanding of their difficulty in seeing clearly.

Treatment for cataracts

Cataracts can easily be removed surgically. However, it all depends on your dog's cataract condition and her temperament.

Dogs must be co-operative and quiet after surgery, especially in the first seven days.

Breeding advice

Cataracts are probably inherited, so affected puppies, their parents and siblings should not be used for breeding.

As some cataracts exist without showing any signs or symptoms, it is recommended that all Lhasas selected for breeding programs have an annual eye-test.

Cherry Eye - third eyelid (nictitating membrane)

The third eyelid is triangular tissue in the inner corner of the dog's eye, which covers part of the eye.

It contains a tear gland and is an important way to protect and 'wash' the surface of the eye. It is sometimes called the *haw* or the *nictitating* membrane.

1) Cherry eye happens when the third eye falls out of its normal place (prolapse).

2) The base of the tear gland flips upwards and can be seen above the border of the third eyelid.

3) The prolapsed gland becomes red and swollen.

4) The condition often occurs in both eyes in Lhasa puppies.

Eversion of the eye cartilage

Eversion of the cartilage supporting the third eyelid is a related condition, which can be seen as a piece of outward-pointing curling cartilage.

It has not been proved that these are inherited conditions, but Lhasas are predisposed to develop it.

Cherry eye - signs and symptoms

Both conditions cause chronic irritation on the surface of the eyes and if untreated, can lead to 'dry eye' (*keratoconjunctivitis sicca).*

Both conditions are seen in younger dogs and are easy to diagnose from the red, swollen appearance of the eye.

Treatment options

Surgery to move the membrane back into its normal position is the usual treatment, although the prolapse may happen again.

Breeding advice

Dogs with this condition should not be bred.

Dry-eye (keratoconjunctivitis sicca (KCS))

KCS or 'dry-eye' is caused by abnormal tear ducts. Insufficient tears are produced to clean the surface of the eye. This causes a serious inflammation of the surface layers of the eyes, which can lead to corneal ulcers and blindness.

Dry-eye can occur as a result of a virus, side-effects from a medication, immune-system disease and it can also run in families of Lhasa dogs.

Signs and symptoms of dry-eye

KCS may develop very quickly or more slowly, in one or both eyes.

1) Dry-eye feels like you have sand in your eyes

2) Dogs will have red, swollen eyes and try to rub their eyes

3) There is often a thick discharge in the eye or around the eye

Your veterinarian can make an accurate diagnosis backed up with a *fluorescein dye test* that checks for corneal ulcers.

Treatment for dry-eye

Artificial tear replacement liquids such as *Cyclosporine* are the first line of treatment. Surgery can be done to transplant one of the salivary ducts to replace the tear duct in affected eyes, but it is not always successful.

Breeding advice

Affected dogs should not be used for breeding.

Eyelash disorders

Normally the eyelashes (or cilia) grow from follicles in the eyelid. Abnormalities of the eyelash are a common hereditary problem in Lhasas. The three types are:

1) **Distichiasis** - extra eyelashes growing from abnormal follicles on the inside edge of the dog's eyelid

2) **Ectopic cilia** - extra eyelashes grow through the eyelid to the inside

3) **Trichiasis** – unusually long eyelashes growing from normal

follicles turn inwards

Signs and symptoms of eyelash disorders

a) With all of these disorders, the signs are irritation of the surface of the eye, (the cornea)

b) If the hairs are coarse and stiff, there will be reddening of the eyes, squinting and noticeable tears in the eyes

c) Your dog may try to paw at, or rub its eyes

d) Corneal ulcers may occur and this will increase your dog's discomfort

e) Ectopic cilia are particularly irritating and likely to cause corneal ulcers

Your vet can diagnose the exact condition and should also do a *fluorescein dye test* to check for ulcers.

Treatment for eye-lash disorders

a) No treatment is required for extra eyelashes that are fine and causing no irritation

b) If corneal ulcers are detected, they can be treated with antibiotics

c) If abnormal eyelashes are the cause, they must be treated or the ulcers will recur

Where there is chronic irritation, with or without ulcers, there are several treatment options.

1) Electro-depilation is suitable for destroying the roots of a few abnormal eyelashes

2) For treating *ectopic cilium*, abnormal follicles can be removed by cryosurgery (chemical freezing)

3) Cryosurgery is the most effective treatment for distichiasis

Breeding advice

To minimize these problems it is best to avoid breeding dogs with abnormal eyelashes

Corneal Ulcers (Corneal Dystrophy)

In corneal dystrophy, ulcers can occur from a long-term irritation of the eye surface (the cornea). In Lhasa Apsos this is usually caused by a combination of abnormal facial features:

1) Protrusion of the eyeball (*exophthalmos*)

2) Inability to close the eyelids completely (*lagophthalmos*)

Affected dogs experience chronic discomfort and often develop ulcers. Dogs with protruding eyes are especially vulnerable to eye injuries from dust, twigs and weeds in open ground.

Corneal ulcers - signs and symptoms

a) Reddening of the eye

b) Increased tears

c) Discomfort with pawing or rubbing the eye

d) Your dog's eyes may not close completely when she is asleep

e) Abnormal pigmentation of the cornea in response to chronic irritation

f) Vision problems

Corneal ulcers develop if eye irritation is not recognized and treated rapidly. Your veterinarian should do a *fluoroscein dye test* to check for corneal ulceration.

Treatment for corneal ulcers

Tear substitutes are given for temporary relief from the irritation, but surgery is the main treatment.

Surgery is usually effective in protecting the eye from further ulcers.

Breeding advice

Any dog that has needed surgical correction for this condition should not be used for breeding, and may not be 'shown' at dog shows.

A responsible breeding program will choose Lhasas with a more normal head and face shape.

Kidney disease (Renal Dysplasia)

Renal dysplasia is an inherited kidney disease that can kill Lhasas pups at 6-12 months old. However, there is a simple DNA test to check for *renal dysplasia* in Lhasa Apsos.

This means you can find out, at any time, whether a dog: i) has the disease ii) is a carrier or iii) is completely free of it.

Amilial kidney disease

A Lhasa pup's kidneys may seem normal at birth, but begin to deteriorate during the first year of life. While the underlying kidney problem varies, the result is usually kidney failure by 5 years of age.

Amilial kidney disease - signs and symptoms

The signs of kidney failure include:

a) the dog drinks more and urinates more

b) poor appetite, loss of weight, lethargy, vomiting

c) pale gums owing to anemia

d) bouts of fever with swelling and pain in the joints, especially the hind-quarters

Note: In young pups, owners may not recognize 'excessive urination' as a symptom of kidney disease immediately. They often think it is the dog's fault for being slow to become house-trained.

Diagnosis of Amilial kidney disease

The symptoms above can have several causes, including other inherited disorders, including a heart or liver defect. Your vet will do blood and urine tests that will find out exactly what is causing your dog's symptoms.

Treatment for amilial kidney disease

Sadly, there is no cure for kidney disease and, with the onset of kidney failure, you should discuss with your vet the right time to put your dog to sleep.

Breeding advice

Affected Lhasas and their parents should not be bred.

Any family members of affected dogs should be screened for protein in the urine. If protein is found in the urine, this is an early sign of kidney disease.

Ear infections

Owing to the large quantity of hair growing in the Lhasa Apsos ears, ear infections are quite common. Therefore, good grooming is important and ear-cleaning should be done at least once a week.

For more information and detailed instructions on how to clean the ears correctly, and instructions for cleaning an infected ear, refer to the section on ear hygiene and grooming, found in Chapter Seven.

Heart disease – heart-valve disease

Dogs of all breeds can develop heart disease, but some breeds are more likely to have specific heart problems than others.

Lhasa Apsos have a greater chance of suffering heart-valve problems. This is known as Chronic Valvular Disease (CVD) or Valve Heart Disease (VHD).

Heart-valve malfunction can lead to heart enlargement or heart failure, with an accumulation of fluid in the lungs or the abdomen. Valve heart disease is a treatable, progressive disease that is common in older dogs.

Heart disease - signs and symptoms

a) Coughing

b) Difficulty breathing

c) Exercise intolerance

d) Fainting

If you notice any of these signs in your dog, it is best to see your vet promptly to identify the cause.

Treatment for heart-valve disease

Treatments for this disease may include medication and a salt-restricted diet. In mild cases there may not be a need to medicate your dog.

Heart-valve illness is often a progressive disease, which cannot be prevented. Regular veterinary checks that include a stethoscope-examination of the heart can often identify this problem in its early stages.

Breeding advice

Mostly affects older dogs that are past the age of breeding.

Hypothyroidism – underactive thyroid

There are two forms of hypothyroidism:

1) Congenital (inherited) hypothyroidism is very rare

2) Acquired hypothyroidism - is not an inherited condition and can be 'caught' from other dogs or the environment

Damage to the thyroid gland reduces the level of thyroid hormones in the body. The 'acquired' form of thyroid malfunction is generally seen in Lhasas between the ages of 4 – 10 years.

Hypothyroidism - signs and symptoms

The gradually decreasing levels of thyroid hormone cause very gradual symptoms. For this reason, the early signs of thyroid problems are often missed.

1) The first symptoms include lack of energy and frequent infections

2) As the disease progresses there may be symmetrical hair loss

3) In some cases there is darkening of the skin

4) The dog's coat may become drier or greasier than usual

Other symptoms include:

a) A slow heart rate

b) Constipation

c) Infertility in males and females

d) Intolerance to cold

e) Lethargy

f) Mental dullness

g) Weight gain

Occasionally, Lhasas with an underactive thyroid may show signs of:

a) A bleeding disorder

b) Diabetes

c) Heart disease

d) Severe muscle weakness linked to abnormalities in muscles or nerves

Congenital hypothyroidism

Puppies with the rare, inherited form of hypothyroidism will have stunted growth and many other abnormalities. Severely affected puppies usually die before weaning.

As the symptoms cover such a wide range, hypothyroidism in Lhasas is difficult to diagnose. Your vet will need to do laboratory tests to be sure.

Treatment for an underactive thyroid

The most common treatment for an adult dog is the drug, Levo-Thyroxine, given once a day for life.

Although it can take up to six weeks to see a marked improvement in your dog's skin and coat, her mood and energy levels usually start to improve within the first seven days.

Dogs on thyroid replacement drugs live a normal life and your vet will check the thyroid levels and adjust the dose if necessary.

Congenital hypothyroidism in puppies

Puppies with congenital hypothyroidism appear stunted in their growth, but they can be treated with Levo-Thyroxine, too. The symptoms are usually completely reversed and the puppy should grow up with normal mental and physical development.

To reverse the early stunting, the condition must be diagnosed and treated very early and not later than 3 – 4 months of age.

Breeding advice

Breeding of affected dogs is not advised. However, the OFA (Orthopaedic Foundation for Animals) maintains a thyroid registry based on assessment of FT4, CTSH and TGAA. This registry helps breeders to select dogs free of hypothyroidism for a breeding program.

Back problems - Intervertebral disk disease (IVDD)

Intervertebral disk disease (IVDD) occurs when the jelly-like inner layer of the spine 'leaks' into the vertebral canal causing pressure on the spinal cord. There are two types of Intervertebral disk disease, Type 1 and Type 2.

Compression of the spinal cord may be slight, causing mild back or neck pain (Type 2 IVDD). It can also be more serious causing paralysis, numbness and incontinence (Type 1 IVDD).

Disc disease is most commonly seen in dogs between three and seven years of age.

Signs and symptoms of IVDD

The signs vary, depending on whether your dog is suffering from Type 1 or Type 2 IVDD.

However, the symptoms of **Type 1 IVDD** are severe and generally develop very quickly over hours or even minutes.

Depending on the area and location of the spinal cord under pressure, there can be:

1) Pain in the neck area

2) Numbness in the limbs

3) Weakness or paralysis in any or all limbs

4) Back pain

5) Clumsiness

6) Inability to walk or paralysis

7) Reluctance to climb/descend stairs

8) Does not want to play

9) Weaving and stumbling gait

10) Yelping when touched, handled or lifted

Type 1 IVDD is a serious disease, which can cause permanent paralysis and incontinence if not treated swiftly. *Strict cage-rest* may ease the symptoms, but surgery is usually needed to relieve the pressure on the spinal cord.

Surgery may restore your dog's normal function, but it is not always successful.

Type 2 IVDD

In Type 2 IVDD, the symptoms tend to develop quite slowly, over a period of several months. There may be pain and weakness, or paralysis, in any or all of your pet's limbs.

Treatment options

Treatment depends on several factors, including the extent and duration of the symptoms. Medical treatment would be a combination of anti-inflammatory drugs with strict cage rest. Vets also need to carry out neurological and X-ray examinations.

If your dog's condition worsens or no improvement is seen within a week or so, surgical treatment should be considered. Surgery is the only way to remove disc material which is compressing the spinal cord.

Breeding advice

It is best to avoid breeding affected dogs or their close relatives.

Loose knees (patella luxation)

The kneecap (*patella*) normally fits into a groove in the thigh bone (*femur*). Loose knees (*patellar luxation*) means the kneecap has slipped out of this groove.

Displacement of the knee can happen occasionally, or continuously. Sometimes, the kneecap pops back into the groove by itself. Other times, your vet may need to push it back.

Your dog will be lame when the kneecap is out of place. Over time, affected dogs may develop osteoarthritis. The mode of inheritance is not yet known.

Signs and symptoms of loose knees

When present, the condition is usually evident in young dogs by around 6 months of age, but if mild it may go unnoticed until the dog is older.

When the kneecap is out of place, your dog will be lame and may refuse to bear weight, or his/her knee may be "locked".

In mild cases, the kneecap may only slip causing your dog to "hop" for a few steps, and then it may slide back into the groove on its own.

In severe cases, the kneecap slips out of place more often, or is never in a normal position. It may not go back into the groove on its own and your veterinarian may need to push it back into place.

Treatment for loose knees and related osteoarthritis

Treatment depends on the severity of disease and whether there are other problems such as osteoarthritis.

Moderate to severe cases require surgery to ensure the kneecap stays in place and to prevent painful osteoarthritis.

With rest and exercise restriction after surgery, the results are usually very good.

Breeding advice

Affected dogs and their parents and siblings should not be bred.

Urinary stones – (*Urolithiasis*)

Urinary stones are created by crystals in the urine combining to form stones (*calculi* or *uroliths*). Stones can occur in any section of the urinary tract, and the cause irritation and secondary infections.

Most end up in the bladder or the urethra, where they can block normal urination. A blockage of this type is a medical emergency.

A DNA test is available to test for this mutation in the many affected breeds.

Signs and symptoms of urinary stones

This problem is generally present from birth. However it takes a long time for crystals to combine into stones. The average age for a vet's diagnosis is between 3 and 6 years.

Stones often end up in the bladder, causing blood in the urine, difficulty in urinating and pain while a dog is trying to empty his bladder.

When a blockage is building-up your dog may only be producing small amounts of urine, but be trying to urinate very frequently. In addition, as toxins build up in the body, there may be:

1) Straining to urinate

2) Vomiting

3) Loss of appetite

4) Weakness

5) Lethargy

Diagnosis for urinary stones

Take your dog to the vet immediately when you start to notice these signs. Diagnosis is made by analyzing the urine for crystals, plus X-ray or contrast radiography. Ultra-sound tests are the most effective way to find any type of stones.

Treatment for urinary stones

Small stones can often be dissolved by medication and changes in diet, to create less acidic urine. In addition, special diets that encourage the production of well-diluted urine, make it easier for a dog to pass stones naturally.

Large stones can be removed through surgery.

What you can do to avoid this problem

Although it is safe when mixed with water, dry food alone should be avoided. Home-cooked meals or tinned food with high water content are recommended.

Provide your pet with plenty of opportunities to drink fresh water to keep the urine from forming crystals. Always give your dog lots of opportunities to empty his bladder, as this stops urine from becoming 'concentrated' and forming stones.

Bacterial urinary tract infections are a common side effect of stones and your vet should treat them quickly. Male dogs are more likely to develop a blockage than females.

Breeding advice

Affected dogs should not be bred, nor should their parents and siblings. Carriers for *hyper-uricosuria* – the tendency to have acidic urine - can be identified through DNA testing.

Von Willebrand's disease – Type 1

Von Willebrand's disease (VWD) is a common inherited bleeding disorder in people and dogs. This disease is usually mild, although Types 2 & 3 are serious, but rare. This disease is caused by a lack of the blood-clotting factor, which in a healthy body acts to stop bleeding.

Dogs with Type 1 VWD have mild to moderate bleeding episodes.

Inherited

Type 1 VWD is the most common form. If either parent has the VWD gene, *some* of their offspring may inherit the disorder. However, not all of their pups will be affected to the same degree.

Signs and symptoms

Many dogs are affected by VWD to some degree. Fortunately, only a small percentage has severe problems. Look out for these symptoms:

1) Prone to nose bleeds

2) Bleeding gums

3) Excessive bleeding when in heat or after giving birth

Most dogs with VWD lead normal lives, with only a few bleeding episodes. This disorder often passes undiagnosed until the dog is 3 – 5 years old.

Always consult your veterinarian before using any over-the-counter medications with your dogs. Painkillers, like Aspirin, can cause internal bleeding in dogs with an undiagnosed bleeding disorder.

Treatment

This condition cannot be cured, but it can be managed under the direction of your vet. Thyroid supplements may help to control bleeding, if your veterinarian finds that your dog has hypothyroidism.

Breeding advice

There is an accurate genetic test to identify:

a) dogs with this disease

b) dogs that are carriers only

c) dogs that are clear of the condition.

Carriers can also be identified through the von Willebrand blood test. Dogs with this disease and carriers should not be used for breeding.

Chapter Eleven: Spaying and Neutering

Spaying and neutering information

If you are not planning to breed your dog, one of the best health decisions you can make for your pet is to have them spayed or neutered.

Having a female 'spayed' means the ovaries and womb are surgically removed by your veterinary surgeon. This procedure is very beneficial for female Lhasas and protects against a number of serious health conditions.

Neutering of male Lhasas means the testicles are removed and this also has important benefits in health, behavior and desire to stay close to home.

Many U.S. states and U.K. counties offer free or low-cost spaying/neutering through vets. This makes this beneficial surgery affordable and easily accessible.

Benefits of having female Lhasa's spayed

Early spaying helps prevent serious infections of the womb and breast cancer, which prove fatal in about 50% of cases in dogs.

Spaying your pet before her first heat offers the best protection from these diseases and gives dogs a longer, healthier life

Will spaying or neutering make my pet fat?

No, that is just a myth. Only a lack of exercise and overfeeding will cause your pet to gain too much weight.

Dogs remain trim and healthy after spaying or neutering as long as owners provide exercise and supervise their food intake.

Spayed females do not go into heat

A spayed female will not have the heat-cycle that attracts unwanted attention from all the local male dogs.

Benefits of neutering males

In addition to preventing unwanted litters, the neutering of male Lhasas prevents testicular cancer - if done before six months of age.

Male dogs stay close to home

An unneutered male will be completely obsessed with finding a mate.

He will try to dig his way under fences and do everything possible to escape. Dogs that get free, risk serious injury from road-traffic and fights with other males.

Neutered dogs do not get lost so often, as they prefer to stay at home and they do not spray urine on your furnishings.

Neutering males saves money

The price of a pet's neutering surgery is far less than the cost of caring for an unexpected litter.

In particular, it avoids the costs of testicular cancer treatment and vet fees for treating dog-fight injuries from dogs competing for a mate.

Chapter Twelve: First Aid for your Lhasa Apso

While it is important to consult your vet, you should also be familiar with the basics of canine first aid. You can learn more about first-aid for your Lhasa online, but this chapter will take you through the basics.

Every home that has a Lhasa should have a first-aid kit. First-aid will reduce the likelihood of having to go to the vet's clinic for minor injuries, such as a scratch that has become infected.

However, the most important reason to learn first-aid is that it will give your dog precious time in a life-threatening situation, until the vet sees her.

A. Important phone numbers

To create a first-aid kit, use a large, lidded plastic container that is easy to keep clean. First of all, tape these important phone numbers inside the container so you will know exactly where they are in a crisis.

1) Your vet's clinic

2) Emergency clinic – along with the address of the clinic

3) Poison Control Center

4) Your breeder

B. First-Aid Kit

There are a number of medications you can keep in this kit, to manage a medical condition and to treat injury or irritation quickly including:

1) Activated charcoal (only use on advice of vet)

2) Antibiotic cream for cuts and scrapes etc.

3) Antibiotic eye ointment

4) Anti-diarrheal medication

5) *Benadryl* for allergies (only use on the advice of vet)

6) Cortisone cream for itchy skin

7) Ear-cleaning solution

8) Eye-wash solution

9) Hydrogen peroxide for use as an emetic if the vet wants you to induce vomiting (only use on advice of vet)

10) Indigestion medicine to help prevent bloat

11) Karo syrup, maple syrup or honey (for constipation)

12) Re-hydration fluid

13) Sterile saline for washing out wounds

14) Wound disinfectant for cuts

Note: Always keep track of the expiry dates of your first-aid medication.

C. Equipment

While you may not feel you need a lot of equipment, you should have the equipment listed below. Sometimes the right equipment means your dog is treated at home and not at the vet's. Or it can save your dog's life.

1) Clean towels and blankets in case of emergency transport

2) Cold packs

3) Cotton balls

4) Cotton swabs

5) Disposable gloves

6) Dog aspirin - only use dog aspirin if and when recommended by your vet

7) Eye Dropper

8) Hemostat clamp

9) Heat packs

10) KY lubricating jelly

11) Magnifying glass

12) Metal nail file

13) Nail clippers

14) Oral syringe

15) Penlight

16) Scissors

17) Styptic powder to stop bleeding

18) Thermometer

19) Tweezers

In addition, you should keep a crate or pet carrier near your first-aid kit for transporting your dog to a clinic, if necessary.

D. Bandages and sticking plasters

Finally, make sure you have sterile bandages, gauze and tape in your first aid kit including:-

1) Band-Aids

2) Square Gauze

3) Non-stick pads

4) First-aid tape

5) Bandage rolls

6) Vet-wrap

Once you have everything on the list, place the kit in an easy to access place in your home.

Guidelines for dealing with an emergency

When you have prepared your first-aid kit and equipment, you may be ready for minor mishaps, but here are some tips for dealing with a real emergency.

No. 1 - Be calm and cautious

Although our first reaction is often one of panic, try to remain calm so you do not communicate your anxiety to your dog. If you are noticeably frightened or anxious, you could cause your dog to react and move about when keeping still is vital to her recovery.

No. 2 - Only move your dog if necessary

In addition, always be cautious when handling your Lhasa in an emergency situation. Moving her could cause further injury or inflict more pain, so only move your dog if she needs to be moved.

If you do have to move her, wrap her up in a blanket first and then move slowly and carefully.

No. 3 - Use your voice and physical touch

Lhasas have a very strong bond with their owners and will react to your voice. If you talk to the dog in a loving and gentle manner, the dog will pick up on your tone and relax.

Touch is even more helpful and if you can stroke your pet gently on the head to help her feel calmer, it will make first-aid easier.

No. 4 - Keep your Lhasa warm

Wrap your dog in a warm, dry towel or apply a warm compress if your dog is unconscious or showing any signs of going into shock. Keeping your dog warm will help to avoid complications arising from her condition.

No. 5 – Stopping blood loss

In the event of an injury with blood loss, apply a clean compression bandage or manually compress the area gently. This will help to slow down or stop bleeding and reduce blood loss.

Remember that what you do in the first few minutes after a serious accident or emergency can mean the difference between life and death in some cases.

First-aid for specific emergencies

i. First-aid for eye injuries

When your dog has an eye injury, it is important to look at the type of injury before trying to treat it.

Dust or similar irritant in the eye

If there is something in the eye, carefully flush the eye with medicinal eye-wash. You may need someone to hold your dog's head while you put the liquid in the eye.

Injury to the eye (with bleeding)

If your dog has injured his eye and it is bleeding, take an eye-dropper of eye-wash and carefully moisten the eyeball. You do not want to flush the eye, but simply to moisten it.

Once it is moistened, apply a sterile compress gently over the eye. This will help to stop the bleeding and keep the eye free from exposure to the air and dust particles/bacteria etc.

Seek immediate veterinarian care after you have administered the first-aid.

ii. First-aid for seizures

There are several medical conditions that may cause one or more seizures to occur. Therefore, if your Lhasa has a seizure, contact your vet as soon as possible.

During the seizure, do not hold your dog. They can be very frightened by this experience and may bite you. In addition to staying clear yourself, remove any objects that he might hurt himself on, such as furniture.

Finally, turn off any type of light or noise stimulation. Lights, radio, TV and music should be turned off, and people should try to stay quiet. While the seizure is happening, time it and write down when it started and when it ended. This is important in case there are recurring seizures.

After the seizure has ended, comfort your dog. Wrap him in a warm blanket and then sit with him until he begins to act normally.

Phone your vet and take your dog in for an examination as soon as possible.

iii. First-aid for heat stroke

With their thick coats, it is possible for Lhasas to develop heat stroke or heat exhaustion. To help prevent heat stroke, do not leave your dog outside in high temperatures and *never* leave a dog in a hot car.

If your dog does develop heat stroke, it is important to follow these steps:

1. Move the dog out of the hot area, indoors or into the nearest shade.

2. Soak a towel with cold water.

3. Place the towel over the neck and head of your dog. Do not cover his eyes, nose or mouth and keep his face clear of the fabric.

4. Repeat the process, wetting the towel down with cold water every few minutes.

5. If you can't get to a vet, pour cold water over the dog's hind legs and abdomen.

6. While you are pouring the water, massage the dog's legs pushing the water downwards and off the dog.

7. This is an important way to keep the water moving, so it carries heat away from your dog's limbs and body.

As soon as you are able to, take the dog to a veterinarian. Heat exhaustion needs to be treated with the help of a trained professional.

iv. First-aid for fractures

There is not a lot of first-aid you can do for a fracture and this is an emergency that will require vet's care. Some people try to create a splint, but this can cause more harm than good.

Instead, take the time to muzzle your dog to keep him from biting. Then make a sling from a small towel to immobilize the fracture and keep her secure.

Do not press on her chest or touch the area where the fracture is. Place a blanket over the body to keep her warm, especially if she is going into shock.

Take your pet to the vet's clinic immediately.

v. First-aid for burns

If the burn is severe or covers a large area, seek medical attention immediately. However, small burns can often be treated at home.

First of all, flush the burn area with large quantities of water for several minutes, to allow the deeper tissue to be cooled adequately. *Non-toxic (if licked-off)* burn relief ointment can reduce pain and a sterile dressing should be placed over the burn.

vi. First-aid for choking

Choking can be a very frightening event for a dog owner and it can happen very quickly. If your dog is choking, act quickly, but be aware that a choking dog is likely to bite you.

1) Carefully grasp her muzzle.

2) Open her mouth and look inside to the throat.

3) If you can see an object causing her to choke, take a pair of tweezers or a hemostat and carefully pull the object out.

Note: It is very important to be careful when trying to remove an object blocking the windpipe, as it is very easy to push the object further down into the throat.

If you are unable to get the object out, seek medical help immediately.

Collapse from choking

1) If your dog stops breathing or collapses, place her on her side.

2) Place your hand on the rib-cage and then firmly strike the rib-cage 3 - 4 times with the flat of your palm.

Repeat as necessary on your journey to the vet.

This technique aims to expel the air from the dog's lungs with enough force to dislodge the obstruction and clear your dog's throat. It is the dog first-aid equivalent of the *Heimlich manoeuvre* for adults choking on food stuck in the throat.

vii. First-aid for shock

This is an emergency that needs immediate medical help. However, shock should be managed as you take your dog to the vet in this way:

1) Wrap your dog in a warm blanket and keep her warm.

2) Lay her down and try to keep her head *level* with the rest of her body.

3) Stay calm and comfort your dog to help minimize her distress.

viii. First-aid for bleeding

If your Lhasa has an injury that is bleeding, it is important to staunch the flow of blood.

Using a thick gauze pad, apply pressure to the wound. The pressure will help stem the flow of blood.

If it is a minor injury, the bleeding will usually stop in a few minutes and you can then move to cleaning the wound.

If it is severe, keep the pressure on the dog's wound. Wrap him in a blanket or use a heat pad to keep him warm.

This will help prevent shock as you take him to the veterinarian for treatment.

ix. First-aid for poisoning

Finally, if your dog is exposed to poison, it is important to immediately call poison control and/or your vet. They will guide you through the steps to take depending on the poison he has ingested.

In the case of some toxins, you may be advised to administer *active charcoal*. In cases of consuming poisons, hydrogen peroxide may be recommended to induce vomiting.

If it is contact through skin or eyes, follow the directions on the container with the poison. Wash the area and flush it with lots of water.

x. CPR for Lhasas

CPR (cardio-pulmonary resuscitation) is a useful life-saving technique you can use if your pet collapses and stops breathing.

If your Lhasa stops breathing, begin CPR immediately. If possible, get someone to drive you to the emergency vet clinic while you are performing CPR.

Do not wait for an emergency to happen, ask your vet to demonstrate how to do CPR for a small dog the next time you visit and be well-prepared for any eventuality.

Here are the basic directions:

1. Put your dog on her side, being careful not to over-extend her neck.

2. Check for any object in her throat that may be blocking the windpipe.

3. Pull your pet's tongue forward gently, so it is even with her teeth and close her mouth. (This is important to stop the tongue slipping back into the throat.)

4. Breath gently into your dog's nostrils. If you are doing it correctly, you will see her chest expanding from your breath inflating the lungs.

5. Lift your mouth from the dog and let her exhale naturally.

6. Then repeat this with one breath from you at roughly every two seconds. Check if your pet has resumed breathing every four to five breaths.

7. If your dog starts breathing, stop doing CPR and let her breath for herself.

Chest compressions

If you cannot detect a heartbeat when you put your ear on her chest, begin chest compressions.

1. Place your pet on a firm, flat surface on her right side.

2. Cup your hands and place them on each side of the rib-cage at the same level as the dog's elbows (above the heart).

If the dog is a puppy or a very small dog, weighing less than 10 lbs., use your thumbs instead of your hands.

3. Squeeze on both sides of the chest and then release immediately, taking about one second each time.

4. If your pet has stopped breathing and does not have a heartbeat, do artificial breathing and chest compressions at the same time. In combination, do one breath for every 3 – 5 chest squeezes.

Note: CPR should only be used when your dog is *not* breathing. Do not administer CPR to a dog that is breathing for herself, as you could cause more harm than good.

The information in this chapter can help in an emergency, but it is not intended to replace the professional care and advice of a veterinarian. Always contact your vet if your dog shows signs of illness.

Chapter Thirteen: Breeding your Lhasa

Breeding your Lhasa is an important decision that needs to be made before you purchase a puppy. Many puppies that make good, healthy adults are not registered as being suitable for breeding.

Puppies registered as suitable for breeding when mature must have a bloodline that is completely free from genetic abnormalities.

Breeding a Lhasa is a constant learning experience and it will help you to know someone who has years of experience. Try to maintain contact with the breeder of your puppy or get to know experts in a Lhasa Apso breed club.

Choosing dogs to breed

The very first thing to do is to choose the right dogs, so ensure that you refer to the Breed Standard set out in Chapter Two.

If you are interested in breeding professionally, you may want to buy a good 'breeding pair'– a male and a female Lhasa. This would cost between £1,000 to £2,000 (or $1,500) for two dogs.

If you can only afford one dog, choose the best female dog from which to breed a litter. You can use stud-dogs owned by other breeders, which is much more economical.

If you have a good female Lhasa, you will likely want to choose a different mate for her each time. That way you can see what kind of puppies she produces with different dogs and different bloodlines.

Serious dog breeders think in terms of generations. Having two or three different litter bloodlines from a bitch would give the best start for the future, if you retain one puppy from each litter for breeding.

In general, when you are choosing a dog for breeding, you should bear the following points in mind:

Health

Dogs should be healthy and in good condition. They should be in proportionate weight for their build and also pass a health test *from your vet*.

They should be free of disease so there is no risk of that disease being passed along to the young. If the vet voices *any* concerns over the health of the dogs, wait until they are in better health or choose different dogs.

Clearances

Clearances are very important to ensure the health of your puppies and the lifelong health of any dog you produce. Lhasas have several hereditary diseases, so the health tests your need are:

a) Eyes Certified by a board-certified ACVO

b) Ophthalmologist

c) OFA or PennHip certification for Hip Dysplasia

d) OFA evaluation for Autoimmune Thyroiditis

e) OFA evaluation for elbow dysplasia is optional in the breed.

In addition to these clearances, you should have the dogs tested for *brucellosis*, which is a sexually transmitted disease in dogs.

Any dog that is being bred should be clear of this disease. *Brucellosis* can cause sterility in both males and females and can cause the mother (*dam*) to abort the puppies.

Registration

Before buying any dog for breeding, you should make sure the dog is registered with the kennel club you desire, or eligible to be registered.

Temperament

A good temperament is as important as health when it comes to breeding and it is a hereditary trait. If you have a dog that is nervous or prone to aggressive behavior it would not be a good idea to breed it.

Bloodlines

Another factor to take into account is the bloodline and how strong the pedigree is. When considering pedigrees for breeding, it is important to have a mentor or someone you trust give you some advice.

You will need to study pedigrees as well as line-breeding, outcrossing and other breeding theories, which are not always easy to understand straightaway.

Age

Age is another crucial matter with dog breeding. Females should be no younger than 18 months of age for breeding and males should not be younger than 15 months of age.

Ideally, males or females are not bred before they have had preliminary X-rays for hip dysplasia, so you can be reasonably sure they do not have this condition. Some health clearances cannot be done until the dog is older.

On the other hand, you should not breed a female after she is 7 years of age. Males can be bred for many years after that; however, the quality and quantity of sperm can be affected by age.

Physical Traits

Finally, you should choose dogs according to their physical traits. While the dogs you select must be good examples of the breed, you should also look at what each individual dog can bring to their future puppies.

For instance, if both dogs have excellent ears according to the breed standard, the odds are very high that the puppies will inherit those ears.

A good coat on a female may be passed on to the puppies, even if the male has a coat that is not as good. A good body shape on the male may be passed on to the puppies and so on. Choosing complementary traits will improve your puppies and your bloodlines, too.

The Lhasa breeding community

While many people enjoy exhibiting their dogs at shows, it is not a *necessity* for dog-breeders. However, showing your dogs, or merely attending shows, does have many benefits for dog-breeders.

It puts you in touch with a community of reputable breeders and allows you to see many different Lhasas and compare traits. It also keeps you informed about dog 'news' and has definite advantages for anyone interested in breeding dogs.

Breeding responsibilities

Before you make the final decision about which dogs to breed, take a moment to remember that breeding is a big responsibility. There is often very little money to be earned when doing it properly and it is a full-time commitment.

While the mother (*dam*) will help with the care, there is a lot to be done during the first 8 weeks (or more) when you are raising puppies at home. In addition, breeders need to be prepared to accept any puppies that are returned for some reason.

Breeding is not for the faint of heart, but one thing is certain: holding a tiny, new-born Lhasa in your hands is worth all the work, money and commitment.

Vaccinations

Before breeding your female dog, make sure she is up-to-date on her vaccinations. Mothers pass temporary immunity to their puppies at birth, protecting them against common dog diseases. Therefore, try to ensure females being prepared to breed have maximum levels of immunity.

In the UK and Europe, it is also recommended that bitches receive the *canine herpes virus* vaccination before breeding.

Canine herpes virus is extremely widespread, affecting up to 90 percent of all dogs.

It is harmless to most adult dogs, but it can sometimes kill new-born puppies. The vaccine is very helpful in protecting new-borns. Unfortunately, this vaccine is not yet available in the United States.

Heat-cycle

When a female dog reaches sexual maturity, she will begin what is known as *a heat*. A *heat* or *heat-cycle* is when the female begins bleeding and will be ready to accept the male within a few days.

For Lhasas, the first heat usually occurs between six months and a year. However, a bitch should never be bred on her first heat or before the age of 18 months to 2 years.

Some females take longer to have their first heat than others. It is not uncommon for a Lhasa to be closer to 12 months or even up to 2 years, before she has her first heat.

The average interval between heat-cycles and coming *in-season* is roughly six months, but there is some variation in frequency. Some dogs come into season every four months and some just once a year.

The signs of being in-season

With heat cycles, there are signs of the heat-cycle before the discharge begins. Often the vulva begins to swell and the female will begin licking her back end and vulva more.

In addition, she may be urinating more frequently and if you have any male dogs in the home, you may notice them paying more attention to her than usual.

The female will begin to have a bloody discharge and this can vary in quantity between females and even between heat-cycles. Some females have very little discharge and others have a lot.

Ready to breed

The bleeding should not last more than 3 weeks and should become paler in color after the first few days. The dog can get pregnant only during the first 2 to 3 days after the heat cycle has started.

Stages of Heat Cycle

When the dog has the heat cycle, she is also *in season*. The heat cycle has 3 main stages:

Proestrus

When your bitch is in the first stage of her heat-cycle, she will reject male dogs.

Oestrus

The oestrus starts from *Day 4* and may last a few days to weeks. During the oestrus period, bitches are ready to mate and will accept male dogs.

Diestrus

Diestrus is the final part of the heat cycle, lasting between 4 - 14 days, depending on the length of the heat-cycle and how long the oestrus lasts.

During this time, the dog will bleed less and will not want to mate.

Natural or Artificial?

When you are breeding, you can choose between allowing the dogs to breed naturally or by using A.I. (Artificial Insemination).

Natural breeding is when you allow the male dog to mount the female and achieve *a tie*. This is more often the preferred way to breed.

Many breeders learn how to do artificial inseminations themselves. However, if you use frozen sperm, you need to have the A.I. done by a specialized, 'reproductive veterinarian'.

Frozen sperm is often shipped by one breeder to another over vast distances, at considerable expense. Therefore, it is more cost-efficient to employ a professional to ensure the insemination does not fail.

With A.I., the sperm is delivered to the cervix through a sterilized tube inserted into the vagina. There are several reasons why you would use A.I. and these are:

1) The chosen stud dog lives too far away.

2) A dominant female that will not allow a male to mount.

3) A sexually inexperienced stud dog.

4) A *persistent hymen* in the bitch.

5) Size incompatibility.

A.I. is less likely to spread an S.T.D., but it usually produces smaller litter sizes. Also, it is important to properly judge when ovulation occurs, which can be difficult and is usually done with progesterone testing by your vet. Many breeders use A.I. with fresh semen, even when the stud dog is on the premises. This is done to avoid any injury to the stud-dog and to avoid any chance of passing disease.

When to Breed

You have the stud-dog, a bitch in heat and you have made the decision to go with a natural tie. This only means you are ready to start breeding *soon* - but maybe not right away.

Breeding times differs from female to female, but if you have the male in your home, you can begin breeding as soon as the female starts accepting him.

Allow them to mate only every other day. This gives the sperm time to recover in numbers and you will get a better sperm count for each mating.

Progesterone testing

If you do not have a male, you can do progesterone testing to try to narrow down when your female is most fertile. Progesterone testing is done with a blood test, but you can also do a vaginal smear, although this is not as accurate.

When using progesterone testing, follow the guidelines of your veterinarian. Testing your bitch is an excellent way to identify if she is ready to be bred. In addition, you can also pin-point the best mating time by observing her behavior.

A female that is ready to be bred will exhibit the following:

1) Vaginal discharge will turn to a light pink or straw color.

2) The female will back up into the male.

3) She will hold her tail to the side (known as *flagging*).

4) She will be playful with the male.

5) She will stand still when the male is sniffing her.

6) She won't attack the male when he tries to mount her.

When you see these signs, your female is ready to be bred. Even with these signs, however, progesterone testing can be more accurate for determining the exact right time for mating to result in a pregnancy.

48 hours before ovulation

There is a spike in the LH (luteinizing hormone) 48 hours prior to ovulation, when the egg is ready to be fertilized. This spike will trigger the progesterone levels to begin rising, signaling the best times for breeding.

After the LH surge and the rise in progesterone, do a natural breeding three days later, for example. The sperm in fresh semen can survive 5 to 7 days in the female dog's uterus.

When to do the A.I. – chilled or frozen sperm

Artificial insemination using fresh, chilled semen can be used *4 days after the rise in progesterone*. Sperm in chilled semen survive 48 to 72 hours after insemination.

Artificial insemination using frozen semen can be used *5 days after the progesterone surge*. Sperm in frozen semen only survives 24 hours once it has been deposited in the uterus by insemination.

The act of mating

When your female is ready to be bred, it is time to let the dogs be together. Never leave them unattended as injuries can occur if the female attacks the male or she becomes scared.

The stud dog will spend some time sniffing the rear of the female and he may begin to lick the vulva. The female will stand still and move her tail out of the way. She will also back into the male.

If you have a maiden bitch or an inexperienced stud dog, you can have success without intervening, but things often go much better if you are on hand to assist. Inexperienced stud-dogs can sometimes be so excited they will mount the wrong end of the girl, for example.

Positioning the female

If you have invested money in a high stud fee or driven a long way to arrange a mating, you or the stud-dog owner may decide to lend a hand. For instance, you can hold the bitch in position or guide the boy in the right direction.

If you have an experienced bitch and/or stud-dog, they usually know what they are doing and things go smoothly and quickly when the time is right.

As the male builds excitement, he will mount the female, wrapping his front legs around the hips of the female. He will begin to thrust against the female and his penis will enter the vulva.

During this action, the bright-red glans penis will come out of the sheath. The penis will extend into the vulva until the dog locks with the female.

Once the lock happens, the male and female cannot be separated. Do not try to separate them as you can hurt both the male and the female.

Once he is locked (or 'tied'), the male will lift his leg over the rear of the female and then turn so they are standing with their back ends together. The penis will bend, but still be inserted in the vulva.

Dogs remain locked for 10 - 30 minutes until the penis loses some of its swelling and is released from the lock/tie.

Myths about becoming pregnant

One myth holds that a female cannot get pregnant if there is no lock/tie. This is not true. When the dog is thrusting, sperm is released.

The fluid that is released when they are locked is very low in sperm and is a lubricant used to push the sperm through the cervix.

Is She Pregnant?

One of the biggest worries that breeders go through is whether a dog is pregnant.

This is very difficult to determine because a female dog goes through the same hormone changes whether she is pregnant or not. In fact, even a female that has not been mated can present the symptoms of pregnancy.

During the first month, you will notice very few signs. The female may have morning sickness and a decreased appetite for food, but some females are not affected at all.

Signs of pregnancy

After the first 30 days, a pregnant dog will begin to show some symptoms including:

a) Nipple growth

b) Darkening of the nipples

c) Decreased appetite early on

d) Increased appetite around week 6

e) Clinginess and other behavior changes

f) Pear shape of the abdomen

g) Weight gain

Ultrasound test

At 30 to 35 days, you can have an ultrasound done to confirm pregnancy. At this early stage it is not possible to tell how many puppies there are.

The gestational period for dogs is between 63 to 65 days after the time of first mating. However, this varies depending on the individual dog.

If you have used progesterone testing, whelping is normally exactly 63 days after ovulation. Even if you have bred your dog late in the heat, you can still count on 63 days from ovulation rather than from the date of mating.

Experienced vets and breeders can palpate a bitch's abdomen and feel the puppies. At 30 days puppies are about the size of walnuts. After this time they can't be felt again for several weeks.

X-ray at 45 days gestation

After 45 days gestation, an X-ray can be done and the puppies can be counted. Sometimes counts are wrong, as puppies may be covered by their siblings.

However, it is important to know how many puppies there are, so at whelping you know when all of the pups have been safely born.

Feeding during pregnancy

During pregnancy, continue to feed your female her normal dog food for the first six weeks.

After this time, you should begin to increase her food, as she needs extra calories to help the pups develop.

Breeders will change to a highly nutritious diet with more calories and sometimes feed pregnant bitches on puppy food to get the balance right.

You can add some pre-natal vitamins for dogs to her diet but do **not** *add any additional calcium* or other supplements at this time.

Once the puppies are born, feed the mother as much as she wants to eat, especially if she has several puppies. She will need the extra calories to produce milk.

Preparing for whelping

The time for whelping the puppies is drawing closer. This is an exciting time, but it is also a busy time for you. It is very important to have all your supplies ready and to begin preparing for the puppies a few weeks before their arrival.

Whelping supplies

The main priority is to have the whelping supplies on hand. These are essential for helping your puppies and mother.

If the birthing goes well, you will need to intervene very little with the labor. In the worst case, you could have to rush your pregnant dog to the vet clinic for an emergency section.

Even an easy whelping can result in puppies in distress, so it is important to have the equipment on hand to help the puppies.

Whelping Box: This should be a clean, square box in which the mother can birth and raise her puppies. You can make the box yourself or purchase a whelping box.

The box needs to be sturdy and of good quality as it will be the puppies' home for the next few weeks.

Blankets: Have a lot of clean blankets on hand for your whelping box. Labor is messy and you have to change the bedding in the whelping box several times during labor.

Newspaper: In addition to blankets, have a large amount of newspaper to put down during the whelping process.

You can sometimes obtain end-rolls from your local newspaper provider. These are plain paper rolls, without the ink, so they will be much cleaner than using newspapers.

Basket: A cloth-lined laundry basket or large plastic container to put the puppies in when the female is birthing another puppy.

Hot water bottles: Towel-wrapped hot water bottles are needed for the basket to keep the puppies warm when they are not with their mother.

Puppies will cuddle up to the hot water bottles if they are feeling cold and move away if they are too warm. You can also use a heating pad, but wrap it with a towel so the puppies do not get burned.

Scales: Have a kitchen scale so you can properly weigh each puppy as it is born. This is a tool you will need throughout the time the litter is with you, to weigh the puppies regularly.

Notebook and pens: Create a notebook that charts the progress of each individual puppy.

Start with the puppy's sex, identifier, date-of-birth, presentation at birth, time born, color/pattern and weight. This will help you keep track of each puppy's health and progress.

Identifier: This can be yarn, puppy collars, or nail polish for their nails. Basically, it is anything you can use safely to identify each puppy.

Use the same color for that puppy throughout the 8 weeks that you have the puppies.

In addition to those items, have the following items available in a kit. Be sure to sterilize all of the instruments, especially the scissors and hemostat-clamps:

a) Sharp scissors

b) Hemostat-clamp

c) Surgical gloves

d) Iodine swabs

e) Alcohol swabs

f) Lubricating jelly such as K-Y

g) Digital thermometer

h) Vaseline

i) Nursing bottles for puppies

j) Liquid puppy vitamins

k) Puppy formula

l) Energizing glucose drops

m) Bulb syringe

Place all of the items into a clean and easy to access container close to the whelping box.

Before Labor

The gestation period for dogs is about 63 days. However, it is important to monitor your dog during the days leading up to the delivery.

Around day 56 to 58, the female should start searching for a nesting site. Encourage her to nest in the whelping box by sitting next to it and calmly petting her. Do not discourage her scratching at the bedding, as this is normal.

In addition, you should start taking her temperature about a week before her due date. The average temperature of your female will be between 99°F to 101°F (37.22°C to 38.33°C). Mark down her temperature each day and, closer to the due date, start checking her temperature several times each day.

About 48 hours before labor, her temperature will have a spike up to about 101.5°F (38.6°C) or higher. Within 24 hours after that, the temperature will drop. Once it drops below 98°F (36.7°C), you will have between 12 to 24 hours before the litter is expected.

First Stage of Labor

After the final temperature drop, you will start to notice a number of signs that indicate your female is going into labor.

For about 2 to 12 hours, your female will become restless. She may start to nest even more than she did before, or she may become very stressed, wanting to wander around the house.

You may see some shivering and she will probably be changing her position frequently. Her eyes will dilate and she will watch you and want to be with you. Try to stay near the whelping box so she can settle in.

She may lose her appetite and it is not uncommon for bitches to vomit at this time. She may also try to go to the toilet and not be able to. This is caused by the pressure building up in her stomach.

If you take your Lhasa outside to go to the bathroom, keep her on a leash and check the spot where she squatted. *It is not uncommon for puppies to be born outside.*

Finally, you may see some mucus being discharged from the vulva.

Second Stage of Labor

During the second stage of labor, your female should start 're-arranging' her bedding even more. You will also notice her looking at her back end more frequently and she may start licking her vulva.

Shivering is more noticeable and she will have episodes where she is panting heavily. You may be able to see mild contractions going across her belly or you may feel a tightening of her abdomen.

Again, your Lhasa may vomit and she may ask to go outside more frequently. Remember to stay with her when she goes to the bathroom to make sure a puppy isn't born outside.

Note: At this time, if the discharge turns to a dark green color, seek medical help. Dark green discharge is only normal *after* a puppy is born.

If it appears before, it can indicate a life-threatening problem for both your bitch and her litter.

Third Stage of Labor

Ensure the room is warm, quiet and calm.

This is the stage of labor when the puppies begin to be expelled or *whelped*. During this time, the contractions will become stronger and you will be able to see them. They will also occur closer together.

Your Lhasa female may vomit during this time and you will notice that she begins pushing and grunting. Some bitches prefer to squat when they have their puppies, others lie down on their side. Let the female decide how she is going to birth the puppies.

As she is pushing, you will see a membrane sac filled with clear fluid containing a puppy come out of the vulva. Puppies are born in their own sac and it may burst while being delivered or as the female breaks it.

Breech births

Puppies are born both front feet first and *breech*, with their tail or back feet presented first. Each puppy is followed by the after-birth. Females often eat the after-birth which contains hormones to stimulate milk production.

After a puppy is born be sure to count each after-birth, to make sure every single one is expelled. A retained after-birth can cause a serious infection and lead to complications for your female.

Puppies are usually born in quick successions of two or three at a time and then you may have a wait of about an hour or so before the next puppies are born.

The process of birthing can last up to 24 hours, depending on the size of the litter.

Weigh and identify the pups

In between the birthing of puppies, weigh the latest puppies to be born, jot down all the notes on each one and place an identification yarn on every puppy.

Problems to look out for

Watching a litter being born is a very exciting thing but make sure you are prepared for any problems.

a) If you find that the female is pushing for longer than 30 minutes without expelling a puppy, contact your veterinarian and follow his advice. It could mean a puppy is trapped blocking the birth canal.

b) If there is a long period of time between puppy births, contact your veterinarian, especially if you are expecting more puppies.

c) When the puppies are born, allow them to nurse from their mother between births.

d) Every time she is ready to push, remove the puppies to your basket. This keeps her from being distracted by the puppies and she is less likely to sit on a puppy or hurt it.

e) Try to let her do the work herself. If you get too involved, you could cause her to stop laboring. Only get involved if she looks like she needs help.

Eclampsia

When the bitch's milk starts to flow during whelping, watch out for the effects of *eclampsia*, which can cause her to experience contractions that convulse the whole body. This can limit her movement and interfere with the birthing of the pups.

The problem is that the demand for calcium is suddenly increased and the parathyroid gland is sometimes unable to respond quickly enough for her needs to be fully met.

If your female becomes fatigued during delivery or seems to have run out of steam, you can give her with some vanilla ice cream for energy.

After whelping, be sure she eats something light, but nutritious and has plenty of fresh water. You can offer her some chicken or broth if she seems to have lost her appetite. She should soon be feeling hungry after nursing the litter of puppies.

The weeks after whelping

It is also important to note that in the weeks *after* giving birth, the gland that regulates the parathyroid hormone (which governs the amount of calcium stored within the mother), can become depleted.

Once diagnosed with eclampsia, the new mother will be prescribed calcium supplements by your vet. In addition, calcium-rich foods such as cottage cheese and goat's milk, will also help her to recover after giving birth.

Raising pups

Raising pups is a fun activity and for the first few weeks, the mother does the majority of the work. She will clean the puppies and feed them.

However, it does not mean that you have nothing to do - you will be very busy with your own chores. Below is a chart of what you need to do with the puppies while they are growing.

Puppy care & development tasks

Week 1

The puppies sleep the majority of the time. When they are awake, they will crawl towards warmth and milk. The puppies have their eyes and ears closed and are helpless at this age.

a) Chart weight twice a day.

b) Trim nails at the end of the week.

c) Handle the puppies daily to check their health and start neurological stimulation.

d) Clean the bedding daily.

e) Monitor the mother and her health.

f) Keep the whelping box temperature about 85°F (29.4°C).

Week 2

Puppies are beginning to move around more and they are awake for longer periods.

a) Trim nails at the end of the week.

b) Hold the puppies in different positions to accustom them to being handled.

c) Monitor the mother and her health.

d) Clean bedding daily.

e) Weigh puppies once a day.

Eyes and ears

Eyes will begin to open at 8 - 10 days and ears will open near the end of week 2 or the start of week 3.

Week 3

Eyes and ears will be open by the end of this week and the pups will be more active.

They will start trying to walk and go to the bathroom without stimulation from mother. They will begin to play and their little teeth will be starting to show.

a) Continue to handle the puppies.

b) Trim nails at end of the week.

c) Begin getting the pups familiar with items such as grooming brushes and combs.

d) Weigh puppies every other day.

e) Monitor the mother and her health.

f) Begin weaning process.

g) Start with milk replacer once a day for two days.

h) Then add a mushy food once per day.

i) Clean bedding daily.

Week 4

During this week, the puppies will be more playful and begin growling. They will also be eating mushy food and nurse occasionally.

Their mother will be resting more and feeding less, but should still be with them a lot. As soon as they start eating foods other than their mother's milk, cleaning up dog mess will be your job.

a) Continue to handle the puppies.

b) Trim nails at end of the week.

c) Begin familiarizing the puppies to other things such as noises and other animals in your home.

d) Weigh puppies every other day.

e) Monitor the mother and her health.

f) Shift the food to be the consistency of porridge and add one extra meal a day.

g) Clean bedding daily.

Week 5

Puppies are more alert and they will be active. You will start to notice pack order and may even see sexual play. Puppies grow quickly during this time.

a) Weigh puppies two to three times each week.

b) Reduce the mother's diet to stop her milk production.

c) Start reducing the amount of liquid in the puppies' food.

d) Continue to handle the puppies.

e) Trim nails at end of the week.

f) Continue getting the puppies accustomed to a range of stimuli.

g) Clean bedding daily.

Week 6

Puppies are developing quickly and showing signs of their own personalities. Mother will spend less time with the puppies this stage.

a) Give each puppy time on their own.

b) Weigh the puppies weekly.

c) Continue reducing the amount of liquid in the puppies' food.

d) Continue to handle the puppies.

e) Trim nails at end of the week.

f) Continue widening the puppies' range of stimuli.

g) Clean bedding daily.

Week 7

Puppies will be able to hear and see fully at this stage. They will be very inquisitive and can get into some problems if you just take your eyes off them for a second.

a) Give each puppy time alone.

b) Weigh the puppies weekly.

c) Puppies should be fully weaned and on puppy food.

d) Continue to handle the puppies.

e) Trim nails at end of the week.

f) Continue socializing the puppies to a range of stimuli.

g) Clean bedding daily.

Week 8

Puppies are at the age where they can start going to their new homes. This is the week when a fear period can occur so make sure you do not stress them too much.

a) Give each puppy some time alone.

b) Weigh the puppies weekly.

c) Trim nails at end of the week.

d) Continue socializing the puppies to a range of stimuli.

e) Clean bedding daily.

f) Start training puppies that have not already left for their new home.

As you can see, raising a litter of puppies is a lot of work. It is advisable to have homes lined up for the puppies before you breed, or at least to know how you will place your puppies.

Lhasa puppies may be highly desirable but it is still necessary to let people know you are breeding a litter. You will want to make sure your puppies are going to good homes after you have put so much work into breeding the litter and raising them.

Most breeders have a waiting list and take deposits on their puppies when they are born.

Chapter Fourteen: Common Terms

So you are interested in the Lhasa Apso? While most of the vocabulary dealing with dogs is the same as with any other animal, there are a few terms that you should know.

In this chapter, we'll cover some common terms that you may encounter as you enjoy life with your Lhasa Apso.

Agility: This is a sport in which the dog handler guides and instructs the dog through a course of obstacles while being timed. Accuracy through this obstacle course is paramount. The dogs must complete the obstacle course without a leash or toys (or food) as incentives. The handler can only use voice, movement and various body signals in order to direct the dog.

Acquired Immunity: when a dog has developed antibodies that enable it to resist a disease. Acquired Immunity is often seen in newborn puppies as they receive antibodies from their dam. It is also seen after vaccinations.

Acute Disease: refers to a disease or illness that manifests quickly.

Adoption: to take an animal or person in as your own. Is commonly used to describe bringing in a dog from a shelter or rescue but can also be used when purchasing a puppy.

Afterbirth: is a term used to describe the fetal membranes and placenta that is expelled after the birth of a puppy.

Agent: a person who trains, works or shows a dog. Also known as a handler.

Albino: a genetic condition where an animal is born with white hair and pink eyes.

Allergen: a particle that triggers an allergic reaction. Found in dog hair, or specifically in a protein that is found in dog dander.

Almond eyes: eyes that have an elongated shape.

Alter: a term used to describe neutering or spaying.

Amble: used to describe a gait where the dog's legs on either side move almost as a pair.

Anal Glands: sacks or glands that are found on either side of the anus. All dogs use the substance secreted by the gland to mark territory.

Anestrus: the period of time between heats in female dogs.

Ankle: found in the hind legs, it is the area between the second thigh and metatarsus where there is a collection of bones. Also known as the hock.

Anterior: the front of the dog.

Apron: refers to longer hair on the chest, also known as the frill.

Arm: refers to the area between the shoulder and elbow of the dog's front legs.

Articulation: refers to the area where bones meet.

Artificial Insemination: used during breeding, it refers to using artificial means to place semen into the bitch's reproductive tract.

Asymptomatic: when a dog has a disease but is not exhibiting symptoms.

Awn hairs: seen on dogs with double coats, it is the section of undercoat that is long and has a coarse texture to it. It should be slightly longer than the downy undercoat but shorter than the outer coat.

Assertion: when a dog has more assertive characteristics than other dogs

Back: the area on the dog that extends from the shoulders to the rump of the dog.

Back crossing: refers to the act of breeding a dog to its parent.

It not recommended to do this. The coefficient of inbreeding should be as low as possible.

Backyard Breeder: a term that refers to a breeder that breeds dogs for profit with little care for the health of the dogs and puppies.

Bad Mouth: when a dog has crooked teeth.

Balance: used to describe the symmetry of the dog as well as its proportion.

Bandy Legs: refers to legs that bend outward.

Barrel: refers to the area around the ribs of a dog.

Barrel Hocks: also known as spread hocks, refers to legs where the hock turns outward, which makes the feet turn inward.

Beefy: when a dog has too much weight in his hindquarters.

Behavior Modification: using training and conditioning to control, alter or teach specific behaviors. Usually refers to aggression, fear and reactivity.

Bitch: a common term used to describe a female dog.

Bite: when a dog places his teeth on something. Also used to describe the position of the upper and lower teeth when the dog has his mouth closed.

Blocky: when the dog has a square like shape to his head.

Blooded: refers to a dog with a pedigree that comes from a good breeding.

Bloodline: the pedigree of the dog.

Blunt Muzzle: when a dog has a square shaped muzzle.

Board: when the dog is placed in a location where the care, feeding and housing of the dog is paid for. Usually used when owners are on vacation.

Body Length: measured from the front of the breastbone to the pelvis to identify how long a dog is.

Booster Vaccination: injections given to a dog to boost the immunity they have to specific diseases. Usually given on a yearly basis.

Bossy: when a dog has shoulder muscles that have been over developed.

Brace: refers to two dogs that are presented as a pair. They should be of the same breed.

Break: when there is a change in coloration between the puppy and adult coat.

Breastbone: the area on the chest where 8 bones connect to form the area.

Breech Birth: the presentation of the puppy at birth. In breech, the puppy comes out hind end first. Breech birth is very common in dogs and does not usually cause a problem.

Breeches: fur on the upper thighs that is longer and fringe like. Also known as pants, culottes and trousers.

Breed: refers to a group of dogs that share common characteristics, traits and gene pool.

Breed Club: refers to a group of enthusiasts dedicated to a specific breed.

Breeder: Any person who produces a litter or breeds a dog.

Breed Rescue: a rescue group that specialized in finding homes for unwanted dogs of a specific breed.

Breed Standard: a description of a breed that describes the physical characteristics as well as temperament to expect in a set breed.

Breeding Particulars: the information about a breeding or litter such as the parents, sex and color of the puppy and the date of birth.

Brick Shaped: a dog that has a rectangular shape.

Brisket: usually refers to the breastbone or sternum. However, it can also refer to the entire chest and thorax of the dog.

Brood Bitch: used to refer to a female dog that has or will be used for breeding.

Brows: the ridge above the eye.

Brush: when a tail has a heavy amount of hair on it.

Brushing: refers to a gait where the dog's legs brush against each other when he walks.

Butterfly: refers to a nose that has only a small or partial amount of pigmentation on it.

Buttocks: the rump of the dog.

By-products: found in food labels, it refers to any food that is not suitable for human consumption.

Camel Back: a dog that has an arched back.

Canid: refers to any animal in the canidae family such as dogs, wolves and foxes.

Canine: a term for dog.

Canine Teeth: also known as eye teeth, the largest teeth found in the dog's mouth. They are long, curved teeth on either side of the mouth, top and bottom.

Canter: a run where the dog has three beats.

Cape: refers to longer hair over the shoulders.

Carnivore: an animal that eats only the flesh of other animals.

Carpals: the bones found in the wrist.

Carrier: when a dog carries a disease that it can transmit to other animals without showing any signs of the disease.

Castrate: when the dog's testicles are removed.

Cat Foot: refers to a foot that is round with high-arched toes.

Cheek: the area between the lips and front of ears just under the eyes.

Chest: the area around the ribs.

Chippendale Front: when the dog's forelegs push out at the elbows on the front legs and the feet turn out.

Chiseled: a dog with a head free of bumps and bulges.

Chronic Disease: refers to a disease that will last indefinitely.

Cleft Palate: when the two halves of the mouth do not fuse properly. It is a birth defect.

Clipping: When a dog's back foot hits the front foot when walking.

Cloddy: a dog that is thick and heavy.

Close Mating: used to describe the act of breeding the same female shortly after her previous litter was whelped. The period of time would be less than 4 months and 15 days.

Close Coupled: refers to a short length of body between the last set of ribs and the hind quarters.

Coarse: a dog that is not refined. Also refers to the texture of the coat when it has a hard or rough texture.

Coat: the fur that covers the dog.

Cobby: a dog with a short body.

Colostrum: the clear to yellowish milk produced by a dam during the first 48 hours after her puppies are born.

Concaveation: when a spayed female produces milk.

Condition: the overall look and health of the dog.

Conformation: a term used to describe the physical traits of a breed.

Congenital: a disease or condition that is present at birth. Congenital problems are not necessarily hereditary.

Coupling: refers to the part of the dog's body that is between the ribs and hind quarters.

Cow-hocked: when the dog's hocks turn inward and cause the feet to turn outward.

Crate: Also known as a kennel, the crate is a container that is used for housing dogs.

Crest: the area on the neck that is arched.

Crossbred: when a dog has a dam and sire from different breeds. Also known as a cur.

Croup: the area around the pelvic girdle.

Crown: the top of the head.

Culottes: fur on the upper thighs that is longer and fringe like. Also known as pants, breeches and trousers.

Cur: when a dog has a dam and sire from different breeds. Also known as a crossbreed or mutt.

Cynology: the study of dogs and canines.

Dam: a female dog that is pregnant or has puppies. Also refers to the female parent or mother.

Dander: the skin that is sloughed off of the dog.

Date of Whelping: refers to the date when the puppies are born.

Dealer: an individual who buys puppies from a breeder and then sells the puppies to others. It is recommended that you avoid puppy dealers.

Deep Chest: A dog or dog breed that has a longer chest or rib cage.

Dentition: the number of teeth in an adult dog, which is 42.

Dewclaw: the claw that is found on the inside of the leg above the foot.

Digit: refers to a toe.

Dock: the act of cutting a dog's tail short.

Dog: refers to canines, however, it is also the term used for a male canine.

Domed Skull: a skull that is rounded.

Domesticated: a term used to describe any animal that has been tamed.

Double coat: refers to a type of dog coat that has two coats; the soft undercoat that provides warmth and the topcoat that provides protection from the weather and terrain.

Down Hairs: the shortest hairs on a dog, which is usually soft and downy in texture.

Dudley Nose: a nose that has no pigmentation.

Elbow: the area on the posterior of the forearm.

Elbows Out: when a dog's elbows turn away from the body.

Embryo: a term used to describe an undeveloped fetus.

Entire: a dog that has not been altered and its reproductive system is complete. Also called intact.

Estrus: the period of a dog's heat cycle when the female is most receptive to being mated. It precedes ovulation.

Euthanasia: the practice of ending life through medical means.

Even Bite: when the lower and upper incisors have no overlap.

Expression: the features of the head and how they look.

F1: the offspring of a direct crossing of two purebred dogs.

F2: the offspring of one F1 parent and one purebred parent. Could also refer to the offspring of two F1 parents.

F3: the offspring of one F1 parent and one F2 parent. Could also refer to the offspring of two F2 parents.

Fang: the canines.

Feathering: Long hair on the ears, tail, legs or body that has a fringe like appearance.

Feral: a dog that has returned to a wild state.

Fetus: the unborn puppy.

Fever: an indication that there is an illness. The body temperature rises to over 103°F in dogs.

Fiddle Front: when a dog's elbows and feet turn out but the pasterns are close together.

Fillers: found in dog food, it is a chemical or low quality, indigestible food that adds weight to the dog food.

Fixed: a term to describe a dog that has been neutered or spayed.

Flank: the side of a dog's body that is between the hip and last rib.

Flat-Sided: a dog that has flat rib, the desired shape is rounded. Sometimes called slab-sided.

Floating Rib: in dogs, the 13th rib is not attached to the other ribs.

Flying Trot: a run where all four of the dog's feet are off the ground for a second on each half stride.

Foster Mother: a female dog that is nursing puppies that are not her own.

Fresh Extended Semen: this is used in artificial insemination breeding where semen is extracted from a male dog and an extender is placed in the semen to expand the lifespan of the semen.

Frill: refers to longer hair on the chest, also known as the apron.

Front: the part of the dog's body that is in the front. This is the forelegs, shoulder line, chest, head, etc.

Frozen Semen: used in artificial insemination breeding, it is semen that is extracted from the male dog and frozen to be used at a later date.

Furrow: an indentation found in the centre of the skull to the stop at the dog's muzzle.

Gait: the pattern of steps when a dog is in movement.

Gallop: when the dog is running.

Gaskin: the lower thigh on the dog.

Genetically Linked Defects: health problems that are passed from parent to offspring.

Gestation Period: used in breeding, it is the time period between mating and birth.

Get: the offspring of a dog.

Groom: brushing, bathing, trimming and caring for the hygienic needs of the dog's coat.

Guard Hairs: the hair that are stiffer and longer than the other hair. Usually protects the dog from the terrain and weather.

Hackles: the hairs found on the back of a dog's neck. It will stand up when the dog is angry or frightened.

Handler: a person who trains, works or shows a dog, also known as an agent.

Haunch Bones: term referring to the hip bones.

Haw: the third eyelid found in dogs.

Head: this is used to describe the front portion of the dog, which includes the muzzle, face, ears and cranium.

Heat: when a dog begins to produce a blood like discharge from her vulva to signal that she is starting her estrus cycle.

Height: height is always measured from the bottom of the foot (ground) to the tallest point on the withers (shoulders).

High in Rear: a dog that has a back end that is higher than its shoulders.

Hock: found in the hind legs, it is the area between the second thigh and metatarsus where there is a collection of bones, also known as the ankle.

Housebreak: training a puppy not to defecate or urinate in the house.

Immunization: when shots are given to a dog to help produce immunity to a specific disease.

Imported Semen: when frozen semen is imported from another country.

In and In: refers to any form of inbreeding in dogs where little consideration is given to the results.

Inbreeding: mating two dogs that are closely related. These include mother to son, daughter to son, sibling to sibling.

Incisors: the upper and lower teeth found at the front of the mouth between the canines. Adult dogs have six upper and six lower.

Incubation Period: the period of time between being infected with a disease and the first symptom appearing.

Interbreeding: breeding dogs that are of different breeds. Also called cross-breeding.

Jacobsen's Organ: this is an organ located in the dog's mouth, specifically on the roof, that functions as a sensory organ for taste and smell.

Keel: the rounded area of the chest.

Kennel: Also known as a crate, the kennel is a container that is used for housing dogs. Also used to describe a place that houses and/or breeds dogs. Many breeders use the term loosely to describe a line of dogs, i.e. "Her kennel produces lovely dogs."

Knuckling Over: a condition seen primarily in puppies where the wrist joints flex forward when the dog is standing.

Lactation: the milk that is produced by the mammary glands from a female dog.

Lead: a term used to describe a leash.

Leather: the part of the outer ear that is supported by cartilage.

Line: the pedigree or family of dogs that are related.

Line Breeding: when a dog is bred to another member of its bloodline such as grandfather to granddaughter, aunt to nephew, uncle to niece.

Litter: the puppies that are produced during a whelping. It can refer to one puppy or several.

Litter Complement: refers to the number of puppies of each sex in a litter.

Litter Registration: a record with a kennel club of a litter.

Lumbering: refers to a dog with a gait that is awkward.

Mad Dog: refers to a dog that has rabies.

Marking: a behavior done primarily by males, although it can be seen in females, where a dog will urinate to establish the boundaries of its territory.

Markings: used to describe the patterns found on a dog's coat.

Mask: when there is dark shading on the face.

Mate: when a male dog and female dog are bred.

Maternal Immunity: seen in newborn puppies, it is a resistance to disease that is temporarily passed from mother to pup.

Measure Out: when a dog's height is larger than the breed standard.

Microchip: a small chip that is inserted under the skin. It contains a code that can be scanned and all the owner's information for the dog can be pulled up. Used as identification.

Milk Teeth: the puppy's first teeth, which will fall out to make way for adult teeth during the first year of life.

Molars: the square, posterior teeth that is used for chewing.

Mongrel: when a dog has a dam and sire from different breeds, also known as a crossbreed.

Monorchid: a dog that only has one testicle.

Muzzle: the protruding section of the dog's head which includes the mouth, and nose.

Natural Breed: a breed of dog that developed without human interference. Sometimes called a landrace breed.

Nesting Behavior: seen in pregnant female dogs or those going through a false pregnancy. It is when the bitch prepares a place to whelp her young.

Neuter: when the dog's testicles are removed.

Nick: refers to a breeding between dogs of two different bloodlines that consistently produces puppies that are desirable according to the breed standard.

Nictitating Membrane: the third eyelid found in dogs.

Odd-Eyed: when one eye is a different color than the other.

Omnivore: an animal that eats both animal flesh and vegetation.

On-Dog Identification: any form of identification that enables people to identify the dog.

Outcrossing: breeding two dogs that are not related but are still of the same breed.

Overage Dam: an older dam that is older than 7 years old when she is bred.

Overage Sire: an older sire that is older than 12 years old when he is bred.

Overhang: a dog with an overly pronounced brow.

Overshot: when the upper jaw protrudes out and the lower jaw is behind the upper jaw when the mouth is closed.

Ovulate: when the ovary releases a mature ovum.

Pants: fur on the upper thighs that is longer and fringe like, also known as breeches, culottes and trousers.

Pedigree: a record of a dog's genealogy.

Pen Breeding: when a breeding occurs due to a male and female dog being penned together. The breeding is not witnessed.

Pile: the dense and soft hair that is the undercoat.

Pinking Up: used to describe a pregnant female dog when her nipples begin to turn pink.

Plucking: the act of pulling out loose hair by hand. Some breeds need to be hand-groomed by plucking.

Purebred: a dog that has parents, grandparents and so on of the same breed.

Quick: the vein that is found in the dog's nail.

Registration Papers: documents from a registry that show proof of breed and whether the dog is purebred.

Scent: the odor that is left in the air or on the ground by an animal.

Scissors Bite: when the lower incisors touch the upper incisors when the dog's mouth is closed.

Season: refers to the period of time when the female dog can be bred.

Secondary Coat: the hairs that are found in the undercoat.

Selective Breeding: when a breeder chooses to breed two dogs together in the hopes of eliminating or achieving a trait.

Septum: the line that is seen between the two nostrils of the dog.

Service Dog: a specially trained dog that works with people who have disabilities.

Show Quality: a dog that is an excellent representation of the breed standard.

Silent Heat: when a female dog goes into heat but shows little or no outward signs that she is in heat.

Single Coat: a dog that does not have an undercoat.

Sire: the male dog, specifically the male parent.

Smooth Coat: a short coat, close to the body.

Soundness: a dog that has both mental and physical health functioning properly.

Spay: a procedure where the reproductive organs of a female are removed. This prevents heat and the female from becoming pregnant.

Spectacles: when there are dark markings around the eyes.

Spread Hock: refers to legs where the hock turns outward, which makes the feet turn inward, also known as barrel hocks.

Stacking: the way a dog stands when being exhibited in a dog show.

Standing Heat: the period during heat when the female will accept a male and can become pregnant.

Stray Dog: a dog that is lost or homeless.

Teat: the nipple of an animal.

Topcoat: the hair that is stiffer and longer than the others. Usually protects the dog from the terrain and weather.

Trousers: fur on the upper thighs that is longer and fringe like, also known as pants, culottes and breeches.

Tuck Up: the waist of the dog where the body is shallower in depth.

Typey: a dog that exhibits the conformation of the breed standard.

Underage Dam: a female dog that is bred before she is 8 months of age.

Underage Sire: a male dog that is bred before he is 7 months of age.

Undershot: when the lower jaw protrudes past the upper jaw while the mouth is closed.

Unsound: refers to a dog that is physically or mentally unable to perform in the way it was intended.

Vaccine: a shot that is given to a dog to help produce immunity to a specific disease.

Variety: when one breed has several subtypes, such as long haired and short haired, but both subtypes can be interbred.

Vent: the anus or anal opening.

Wean: the process of switching a puppy from milk to solid foods.

Weedy: a dog that lacks the musculature that is described in the standard.

Whelp Date: the date when the litter is born.

Whelping: this is the term used to describe a dam giving birth.

Withers: the top of the shoulders of the dog.

Zoonosis: a disease that can be passed from animal to human.

Chapter Fifteen: Rescue Dog Adoption

Lhasa Apso 'rescue dogs' for adoption

If you feel that the Lhasa Apso breed would suit you, but do not have enough free time to devote to training a puppy, why not adopt a 'rescue dog'?

The advantages of this include not having to 'house-train' or fully train a new pet that has probably come from a good home. The disadvantage is that some 'rescue dogs' are available because they have been neglected by their former owners.

However, that is not so likely with a small, pedigree dog such as the Lhasa Apso. Most Lhasas are given up for reasons that do not reflect badly on their former owners, nor the care and affection they may have shown to their pet.

However, the background of each rescue dog can be checked and discussed fully with the staff at a rescue shelter. Their whole focus is to find new owners who can be the best match, for their dogs; people who will provide the love and care required for each individual dog.

Resources

Lhasa Apso Club U.K. National Breeders List

This page is for anyone wishing to talk to fully paid-up members of the Lhasa Apso Club in their area when looking for a well-bred puppy.

Contacts on this list may not have puppies available immediately, but are happy to be contacted.

East of England

Helen Bell, (Vallena) - Based near Luton

Tel: 01582 483589/486212

Email: helen@vallena.co.uk

Mrs M Sutcliffe & Mrs G Fleet, (Newcliffe) - Based in Suffolk

Kennel Club assured Breeder

Tel: 01728 603706

Email: newcliffe888@hotmail.co.uk

Belinda Yaxley, (Dardanelles) - Based in Norfolk

Kennel Club Assured Breeder

Tel: 01603 893050

Jon Norris, (Damjoz) - Based in Norfolk

Kennel Club Assured Breeder

Email: jonhobland@hotmail.com

Mrs G Free, (Marpori) - Based in Suffolk

Kennel Club Assured Breeder

Tel: 01728 830424

Email: gail.free07@btinternet.com

Mr. & Mrs. G. Leaver, (Shogandale) - Based in Ipswich

Tel: 01473 741613

Email: gordonleaver@sky.com

Miss N. Crummey, (Nickanda) - Based in Luton Kennel Club Assured Breeder. Tel: 01582 754159

Mr. C. Andersson, (Tantra) - Based near Peterborough

Tel: 01354 659838

Mrs. S. Pointon, (Ballito) - Based near Sleaford

Tel: 01529 241396

Email: s.pointon@btinternet.com

Mrs. I. Plumstead, (Showa) - Based in Norfolk

Tel: 01603 416282

Email: Plumsteadir@aol.com

Mrs. C Walker, (Shigatse) - Based near Cambridge

Tel: 01354 638488

mailto:shigatse1234@sky.com Email

Mrs. Kellie Harmer, (Remrah) - Based in Cambridgeshire

Kennel Club Assured Breeder

Tel: 01945 772183

Email: dick_kel@hotmail.co.uk

Midlands

David and Jacquie Chalmers, (Chethang) - Based near Doncaster

Tel: 01302 849900

Email: chalmersd@rocketmail.com

Mrs. M. Lewis, (Deelayne) - Based near Coventry

Kennel Club assured Breeder

Tel: 02476 615626

G. Holland and C. Bloomfield, (Vaderlands) - Based near Wolverhampton

Kennel Club Assured Breeder

Tel: 01902 862946

Mr. Peter Moorby - Based between Sheffield and Nottingham

Tel: 01909 475578

Email: peterswansdown@aol.com

Northern England

Miss A.M. Cassidy, (Exephials) - Based near Leeds

Tel: 01132 860463

Mrs. H. Horne, (Chanceinn) - Based in East Yorkshire

Kennel Club assured Breeder

Tel: 01262 409135

Email: chanceinn@hotmail.com

Mrs. C. Lawson, (Rishlyn) - Based near Warrington

Tel: 01925 713444

South East England

Mrs. Brenda Bushell, (Jamikasoka) - Based in Kent

Kennel Club Assured Breeder

Tel: 01634 724170

Mr. and Mrs. D. Lock, (Littondale) - Based in Hampshire

Kennel Club Assured Breeder

Tel: 01730 891049

Email: Littondale@live.co.uk

Mrs. J. Waghorn, (Sukisha) - Based in Kent

Tel: 01732-871528

Email: sukisha@btinternet.com

Mrs. T. Wiehe, (Lisimo) - Based near Hornchurch, Essex

Tel: 01708 446290

Email: teresa@lisimo.biz

Mr Dungate & Mr Minton, (Forochel) - Based near Hailsham

Kennel Club Assured Breeder

Tel: 01323 841204

Email: forochellhasas@aol.com

South West England

Mrs. S Bedford, (Sangchenla) - Based near Newbury

Tel: 01635 253605

Email: sarah_bedford@hotmail.com

Jane & Allan Paradise, (Shardlow) - Based in Gloucestershire

Kennel Club Assured Breeder

Tel: 01452 312668

Email: jane@shardlow-squad.co.uk

Mrs. Dorothy Quelch (Ardquin) - Based near Hereford

Kennel Club Accredited Breeder/Assured Breeder

Tel: 01989 562515

Email: ardquinapsos@yahoo.co.uk

Scotland

Kimberley McCosh & Chris Logan, (Spyanki) - Based in Wishaw, N. Lanarkshire

Tel: 01698 381325

Wales

None at the time of publication of this guide

Northern Ireland

Sarah Matthews, (Tasarnia) - Based in Co. Down

Tel: 02892 611317

Email: tasarnia@tiscali.co.uk

Lhasa Apso Club U.S. Breeders List

The American Lhasa Apso Club - ***https://www.lhasaapso.org/*** is the best place to consult for up-to-date details of registered breeders and rescue shelters in all the different states.

Here is a list to get you started:

Alberta

Shirley Clark, Apsolutely, Red Deer, Alberta, 403-887-3421, cre8sal@agt.net

Arkansas

Patrick & Jeannie Clary SengTru Lhasa Apsos, Arkadelphia, AR 870-403-7256, jclary1500@gmail.com

Arizona

Kathie & William Ruffner, Spindrift, Mesa, AZ, 480-456-8842, kathie@lhasaapsos.net

Boni Ives, BonMi, Scottsdale, AZ, 480-219-5511, bonmi@centurylink.net

British Columbia

Patricia Furmedge, Furchila, North Vancouver, BC 604-985-9470, Nordvan@aol.com

Arlene Miller, Desiderata, North Vancouver, BC, 604 929-3570, arlenemiller@telus.net

California

Jan Lee Bernards, Summerhill, Valencia, 661-259-3229, jan@summerhillec.com

Susan Vaughn, Grace Lhasas, Newport Beach, CA, 949-636-1990, slmvb@comcast.net

Linda Crabill Byrne, Shangri, Monterey, 831-647-0449, lindabyrne1@comcast.net

Barbara Dwelly, Rockcrest, Novato, 415-897-4000, the.crest@verizon.net

Pat Keen-Fernandes, Hylan Sho Tru, Knightsen, CA, 925-679-8676, shotru@comcast.net

Wendy Harper, Krisna, Granit Bay, CA, 916-899-6550, wendyharper@sbcglobal.net

Darby McSorley, Rumtek, Los Gatos, 408-354-8677, darbymcs@aol.com

Cathy Sarantis, Tara Mi Kiralyi, Citrus Heights, CA, 916-725-5150, taramicls@yahoo.com

Beverly Simms, Merced, 209-722-3235, Lhasamagic@aol.com

Yvette Supriano, Duskra, Roseville, duskra@aol.com

Sherry & Ben Swanson, Shoyu, Dublin, 925-833-9257, Shoyulhasa@aol.com

Ellen Voss, Galaxy, Los Angeles, CA, 323-658-8291, galaxylhasas@yahoo.com

Nancy Wilcox Hollister 831-637-2107, nancycwilcox@yahoo.com

Colorado

Debby Rothman FFT (Fleetfire Timbers) and Kunza Conifer, CO 303-674-0136, LhasaLhady@aol.com www.FleetFireTimbers.com

Fran Strayer NuSeng Lhasa Apsos Littleton, CO, 720-981-8600, fmstrayer@aol.com

Susan Vaughn, Grace Lhasas, Fort Collins, CO, 80525 (970) 472-9519, slmvb@comcast.net

Delaware

Linda Kendall Smith, Orlane, Wyoming, DE, 302-697-6936, Website: orlanelhasa.com, orlane2@verzion.net

Florida

Phyllis Huffstetler, Phuffs, Belleview, FL, 352-357-7782, phuffstet@aol.com

Indiana

Leslie Baumann, ShiSedo, Valparaiso, IN, 219-462-9520, ltbaumann@comcast.net

Illinois

Joyce Johanson, Joyslyn's, Macomb, IL, 309-837-1665, jkjohanson@wiu.edu

Diane Selmer, Majik, Oswego, IL, majwiz@aol.com

Maryland

Norma Perna, Shellinor, Potomac, MD, 301-299-6262, shellinor@hotmail.com

Beverly A. Drake, Misti Acres, Glen Arm, Maryland, 410-592-6636, bdrake216@comcast.net

Don & Marge Evans, Baywatch, Huntingtown, Md, 301-494-3647, margievans@msn.com

Elaine King, Bodnath, Silver Springs, MD, 301-585-3327, elaineking722@verizon.net

Gina Pastrana, Baywind, Davidsonville, MD, 410-798-0638

Massachusetts

Stephanie Kodis, Mokiema, Canton, MA, 781-828-0553, mokiema2@aol.com

Julie Luther, Cespa Lhasa Apsos, Franklin, MA, 508-528-3031, cespa@comcast.net

Mary Powers, Mokiema, Canton, 781-828-0553, mokiema2@aol.com

Janice M. Tilley, Solitude Lhasas, Oxford, MA, 508-987-1068, Solitudela@aol.com

Michigan

Cheryl Zink, Ming, Westland, Michigan, 734-728-5810, cherylazink2@aol.com

Minnesota

Julie Timbers, FFT – FleetFireTimbers, Cottage Grove, MN, 651-334-3042, TmbrLhasas@comcast.net, www.FleetFireTimbers.com

Melissa Torgerson, MeLou, Stillwater, MN, 651-283-7571, MeLouLhasas@yahoo.com

Mississippi

Sue Cannimore, Red Fox Lhasas, Terry, MS, 39170 601-853-7763, redfoxlhasas@yahoo.com, http://www.redfoxlhasas.com

Missouri

Sandra South and Tom Sorth, Windwick Imperial, MO, 636-464-1423, windwick@att.net

Polly (Pauline) Naumann, Riverview St. Louis, MO, 63138 314-653-6339, RViewlhasa@aol.com

North Dakota

Marsha Susag, MLS Dakota Lhasa Apsos, Fargo, ND, 58102 701-235-6211, dmsusag@msn.com

New Hampshire

Rita Cloutier, Ransi's, Milford, NH, 603-673-0042, lhasas@hotmail.com

New Jersey

Bobbie Wood, Anbara Cranford, NJ, 908-272-8995, Anbara@comcast.net

New Mexico

Sandy Devlin, San-Dhi's, New Mexico, 505-280-8297, slhasa@aol.com

North Carolina

Catherine Marley, Kai-La-Sha, Waxhaw, NC, 704-256-9095, kailasha@lhasa-apso.org

Ohio

Marilyn J Lucas, Cozmos, Cincinati, OH, 513-385-2394, cozmosknls@aol.com, www.cozmoslhasaapsos.webs.com

Sami Payne, Samara, Sunbury, OH, 740-965-2801, SamaraPayne@aol.com

Oklahoma

Linda McCutcheon, Rushmar, Marlow, OK, 580-658-6856, rushmar@sbcglobal.net

Oregon

Nan Damberg, Pawprints, Boring, OR, 503-663-2551

Ontario

Sue & Ron Decleir, Idecleir, Burlington, ON 905-634-6874, idecleir@sympatico.ca

Pennsylvania

Carol Aitken, CPC, Chadds Ford Lhasas, Chadds Ford, PA, 610-388-0587, aitken@400search.com, www.chaddsfordlhasas.com

Kathy Fallon, Moja's, Feasterville, PA, 215-322-2808, mojaslhasasandmaltese, @verizon.net

Jerri McDonough, MCD'S, Warrington, PA, 18976, jmcdlhasa@verizon.net

Kathaleen Kalavoda, Kories, Bath, PA, 610-703-7382, chklhasa@hotmail.com, http://www.korieslhasa.com

Kathleen Walcott, Floral Hill, Hermitage, PA, 724-962-2239,

kathleenwalcott@verizon.net www.floralhill-lhasaapsos.info/

Tennessee

Peggy Huffman, Tara Huff, Collierville, TN, 901-861-0666, tarahuff@worldnet.att.net

Kathy A,. Miller, Rosewood ROM, Lebanon, TN, 615-444-1087, Rosewoodla@yahoo.com

Carla Varney, Hi Tide, Jacksboro, TN, 423-562-5741, hitide@infionline.net

Texas

Marie Allman, Chiyoko Freeport, Texas, 979-233-

1853, wjallman@hal-pc.org

Lois & Miki DeMers, Conroe, 936-321-4628, BIS4TTS@aol.com

Robin Fisher, Ku-Ther, San Antonio, TX, 210-525-8763, robin@satx.rr.com

Sandy Fluhart, Odie Lhasas, Magnolia, TX, 281-356-7157,

odielhasas@sbcglobal.net www.odielhasas.com

Carole Merz, Creeksong, Seguin, TX, 830-305-4700, crksng@sbcglobal.net

Ronny Junkins, Jaron, Dallas, TX, 972-931-7224, jaronslhasas@hotmail.com

Lee Nagel, San Antonio, 210-344-9079

Nancy Stephens, Kha Thi, Lake Jackson, TX, 979-297-7655, NANStephens@hotmail.com

Clay Williams Allen, TX, 972-727-8968, K9clay@tx.rr.com

Utah

Tom & Marsha Worlton, Eagle Mountain, UT, 801-228-1691, mworlton@yahoo.com

Virginia

Susan Giles, Kinderland Ta Sen, Manakin-Sabot, VA, 804-749-4912, ssgiles@aol.com

Wisconsin

Lavonne Bennett, Madison, WI, 608-274-0647,
jonlavon@tds.net

Jan and Dean Graunke ,Golden Tu, Manitowoc, WI, 920-683-2245, goldentu@lakefield.net

Karen Schlais Medford, WI, 715-748-9675, k_schlais@yahoo.com

Lynn Replogle Madison, WI, 608-221-4332,
woodlyn@tds.net

Washington

Barbara Corbett, Tora, Carnation, WA, 425-788-7985,
barbcorbet@aol.com

Cassandra de la Rosa, Suntory, Olympia, WA, 360-357-6743, dlrcas@msn.com

Becky Ann Hughes, OB-One, Snohomish, WA, 360-668-2842, becky@wmhughes.com

Ann Lanterman, Kian, Sammamish, WA, 425-868-0276, kianlhasas@aol.com

Tia McLaughlin, Kumi, Puyallup, WA, 253-353-1284, ShoPups@aol.com

Susan Whitakerhill, Karakal Lhasa Apsos, Kennewick, WA, 509-736-6012,

lhasa.apsos@yahoo.com, karakallhasas.com

Photo Credits

All photos found within this book, including the cover photo have been provided by Belinda Chang.

Thank you Belinda – it was a pleasure working with you.

Lightning Source UK Ltd.
Milton Keynes UK
UKHW020756040219
336707UK00012B/920/P